Each Day Fortune Gave Me...

A Brief Autobiography
RONALD J RAYNER

BIRCH LEAF BOOKS

birchleafbooks.co.uk
Specialising in family and local histories

William Bramhill and Stephen Rayner acting as Birch Leaf Books
80 Mile End Road
Colchester
CO4 5BY

www.birchleafbooks.co.uk

This edition October 2010
First published October 2010 in Great Britain by
Birch Leaf Books

Copyright © Ronald Rayner
Ronald Rayner asserts the moral right to be
identified as the author of this work.

ISBN 978-0-9564677-0-6
Printed and bound by Blurb www.blurb.com

CONDITIONS OF SALE
This book is sold subject to the condition that it shall not, by way of trade
or otherwise, be lent, resold, hired out or otherwise circulated without the
publisher's prior consent in any form of binding or cover other than that
in which it is published and without a similar condition including this
condition being imposed on the subsequent purchaser.

All rights reserved. No part of this publication may be reproduced,
stored in a retrieval system, or transmitted, in any form or by any means,
electronic, mechanical, photocopying, recording or otherwise, without the
prior permission of the publisher.

Dedication

Dedicated to all my family — past, present and future

Acknowledgements

Without the help and encouragement of my daughter Marion it is doubtful if my life story would ever have been written and printed. Marion converted my scribblings into type, made constructive criticism and offered suggestions. I am indebted to her and thank her sincerely. My daughter Brenda had a better memory than my own at times, and sister Jean helped greatly with family matters.

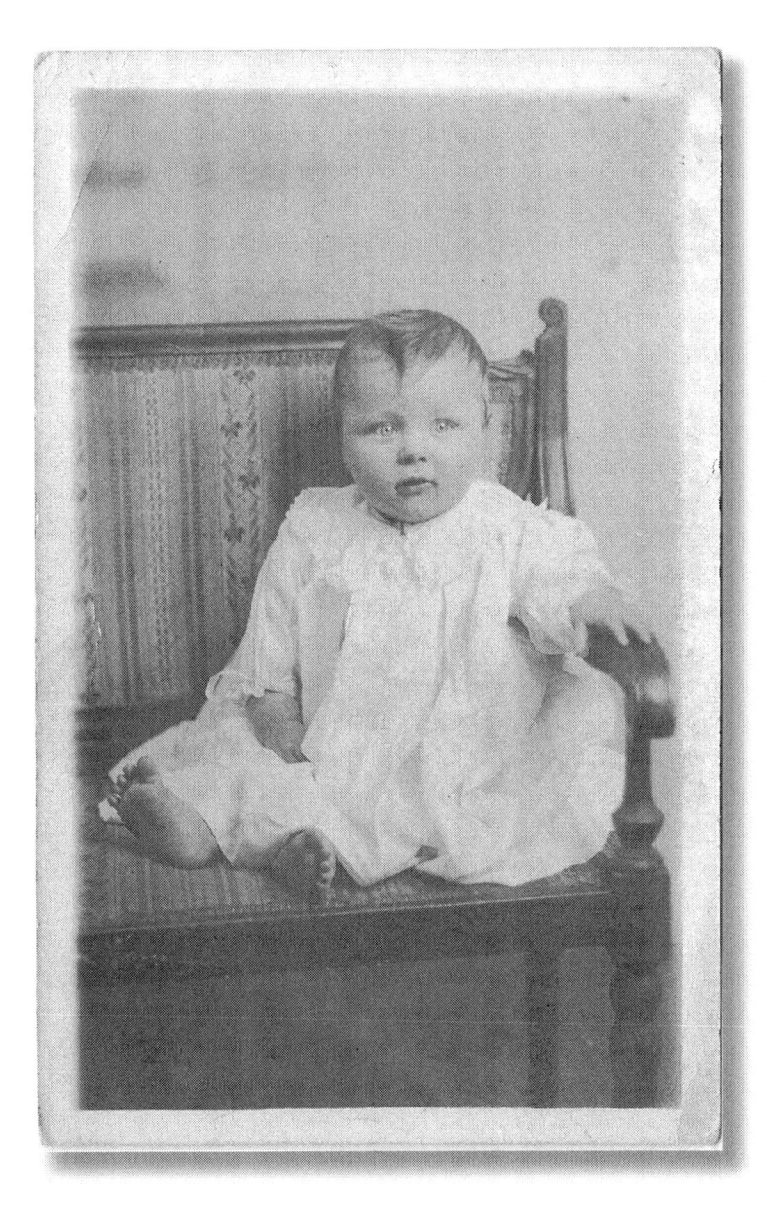

Age of innocence: me as a baby

My family: Aunt Grace, Grandfather Nickells, Uncle Sam, Aunt Hilda, my Mother, Aunt Louie, Grandma Nickells and Uncle Gordon

Childhood home – No 136 Greenstead Road, Colchester, house on right of picture, in 2009

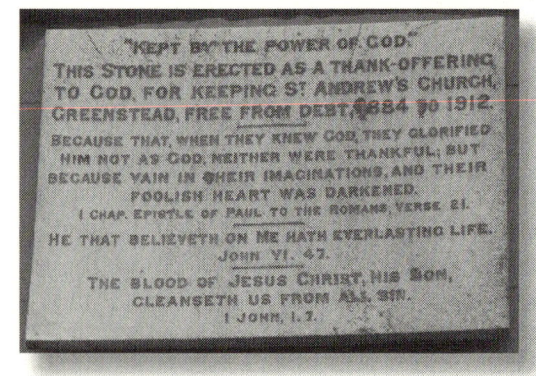

The marble slab over the front door of Providence Cottages, thanking God for keeping St Andrew's Church free from debt

Write a book? Me?

During a family meal at the Red Lion, Thorrington, conversation turned to some aspect of my past — war service, I think — that led my daughter Marion to suggest I put pen to paper.

I had never considered my life as being of interest to others but doubts were banished a few weeks later when a lecturer on family histories said such stories are of interest to many people and organisations including universities and libraries.

So here it is: thoughts from the past, memories, one thing following another, an incident remembered that had lain forgotten through the years. It is a tale I hope will interest you.

To describe my life I need only a few words: enjoyment and grateful thanks to all who made it happen and let me share in their love and affection. Like the weather, life has its sunny times and its storms but I have no complaints, apart from losing six years to the war – and even that experience was not completely negative.

As Horace, the Roman poet said: "Each day that fortune gives you, be it what it may, set down for gain."

My Family

Grandparents

Both my grandfathers died before I was born so what I know of them I have heard from others. Grandfather Rayner came from Sudbury and was an engine driver. Further back in time the Rayners came from Bures Hamlet and were agricultural workers. Grandfather Nickells was a market gardener and carter. The market garden was behind the family home in Greenstead Road, Colchester, but is now largely beneath St Andrew's Avenue, part of the bypass built in the early 1930s.

Grandmother Nickells had four sisters living during my early years: Alice who lived two doors away, Emma in Ipswich, Louie in Colchester, and Grace who lived with us. Great-aunt Louie lived near East Gates, and with her son Arthur she ran a general store and delivery business. She was always known as Aunt Louie and Arthur as uncle, although strictly not correct.

Parents

Father had five brothers and two sisters but I only knew Harry, Albert and Ada, and met them quite often. Harry lived five doors from us in Greenstead Road, Albert at the top of Hythe Hill and Ada near the Recreation Ground along Port Lane — all within a mile or so. Mother had two brothers, Sam and Gordon, and two sisters, Hilda and Louie. Sam lived with Grandmother, Gordon lived at Old Heath, Colchester, and Hilda lived in London during my early years but later came home and lived with Grandmother. Louie (not to be confused with Great-aunt Louie) ran an off-licence in London with her husband Jim.

Brothers and sisters

I had one brother and two sisters. Joan was born in December 1921, two and a half years after me. She served in the Army during the war, married Bob, a soldier, and moved to his home town of Newcastle. Ken was born in January 1925, he served in the Army in Egypt until demob at the end of the war. As an engineer his peacetime job took him all over the country and while in Lincolnshire he met and married Marion, an innkeeper's daughter, and settled in Gainsborough. Jean was the youngest, born in April 1928, and she was too young for war service. She married Peter and has always lived in Colchester. Jean and Peter lived with Mother all their married life and did a wonderful job of looking after her, particularly later on — and she lived to be 89.

Wives, children and grandchildren

I met Sally in 1943 and we had two girls, Brenda and Marion. Sally and I divorced in 1963 and she died in 2003. Brenda is married to Ken and they have a son Ben. Brenda also has Craig and Charlotte from her first marriage and it is a comfort to me that they are all a happy family. Marion is married to John and they have twins Simon and Paul.

My second wife Megan and I had a wonderful time together until 2003 when she died following a long period with Alzheimer's disease. Her three children — Ann, David and Stanley — accepted me as Dad and we have had a rewarding and loving relationship. Through them I have 'grandchildren' Hannah, Stephen and Kirsten, and Owen. I am blessed with a loving and caring family which is now spread across the globe. If we cannot meet we keep in touch by phone or e-mail but not often by letter these days!

And forwards…

At the time of writing I have a growing number of great-grandchildren. Of course I think my family are special and I thank them for the love and happiness they have given me. What more could anyone ask for? I have been blessed.

Sister Joan and me, pictured in 1922. My suit was brown velvet.

Take-off

June 15, 1919, was an auspicious day for four people in particular. Alcock and Brown became the first men to fly the Atlantic Ocean in one hop, and John and Flora Rayner became proud parents of their first child — me.

I was born at what is now 140 Greenstead Road, Colchester, apparently just in time for Sunday lunch on a hot, sunny day. The house was where Aunt Alice lived and mother was there because the two pairs of semi-detached houses Grandfather was having built next door were not yet finished.

Shortly after my birth we moved into our new house. We were in Abstinence Cottages; the other pair was Providence Cottages. A marble slab over the front door of 136 still intrigues passers-by. The reason they got the names, so I have been told, arose from a fright that Grandfather's brother had. He was partial to the comforts of the Buck's Horns public house farther up the road and, wending his way home one dark night, was shocked to hear the devil calling to him. What the devil said I do not know but from that night on he never touched a drop. Grandfather decided to extol the two virtues when he named the cottages.

My childhood was spent in a situation that I think would be hard to find with today's dispersed families. Three doors away was my maternal grandmother and Aunt Hilda and Uncle Sam who were Mother's sister and brother. Two doors away was Great-aunt Alice who was grandmother's sister, and five doors away Aunt Eva and Uncle Harry, who was Father's brother, and their two children Jim and Dinah. We also had Great-aunt Grace living with us. She was deaf and dumb but this in no way stopped her from being an integral and active part of the family. I still remember most clearly the way she used to scold me if I did something wrong. The stamp of the foot, the wagging finger and the sound, somewhat like a growl, that she could make when really provoked. On the other side of the coin, her pleasure and thanks were ample rewards for any efforts I made to please her. Often was she my champion when I was in trouble with Mother or Father. I have often thought about her dumbness and wondered if it was a result of being totally deaf. In her Victorian childhood it was probably thought she couldn't be taught to speak.

Throughout my early years I moved freely from one relative to the other as I pleased, but was always aware that a telling-off was likely from any of the family if it was deserved. I spent a great deal of my early years, certainly up to the age of seven or eight, with Grandmother, and slept there most of the time. I still vividly remember lying in her double bed in the front bedroom before falling asleep. Bedrooms were not heated and in the winter I was allowed to undress and change into my bedclothes in front of the living room fire before going upstairs. There was no quick jump into bed: I had to kneel at my bed-side, head down between my hands and say my prayers. Two were usually sufficient in winter and they were varied to keep me alert. This routine might seem somewhat hard but I never thought it so. I loved my Gran, she was such a gentle, caring and loving person: strict when necessary, but a warm safe haven when things went wrong.

The gas-light from the other side of the road cast a ray

of light across the ceiling through the open curtains. Basil the lamp-lighter had lit that lamp on his round at dusk and would be back later to put it out. The street lights did not stay on all night. The occasional car or lorry would pass and a beam of light would cross from one side of the room to the other, and to lull me off to sleep would be the sounds of the railway trucks being shunted at the Hythe, which was a busy station.

If for any reason I was troubled by the dark I was allowed a small oil-lamp on the bedside locker. To soothe any chesty coughing, a saucer of vinegar with sugar cubes at the side was placed by the lamp. If coughing was bad, a cube was dipped in the vinegar for me to suck. Not that I could help myself to them — they were doled out by Grandmother, only when strictly necessary.

Uncle Sam lived with Grandmother and I think he was her eldest son. He remained a bachelor, was occasionally crusty, but I liked him. He was a drayman with Colchester Brewery and one day he took me on a delivery to Wivenhoe. I still remember the pleasure and fascination of sitting beside him, high up behind those four (or was it six?) great horses. Uncle Sam used to bring home magazines from where he worked for the Town Council — I suspect they were being thrown out and he rescued them. Grandmother was annoyed and used to push them out of sight under the sofa cushions. They were wonderful windows on the world for I was an avid reader; I cannot remember a time when I could not read. National Geographic and The Strand Magazine were two titles that come to mind. It was all very innocent, there were no 'top-shelf' magazines.

A great part of my early years was shared with Grandma Nickells and with her I enjoyed trips to London on the train to visit Aunt Louie and Uncle Jim at the off-licence in Neasden Lane. I had three cousins there, Gordon, Win and Edward (Ted). Ted was a year older than me and he often used to stay with Grandma during the school holidays. We got on well together but occasionally you were reminded of your rusticity living out in the country, far from the city life of London. In the summer of 1924 Grandmother took me up to London and with Aunt Louie we visited the British Empire Exhibition at Wembley. I can still remember some of it and for many years we had a cup and saucer with the Wembley Exhibition emblem on them. Sadly they got lost after I left home for war service.

Being the eldest of four children in the family I suppose I should remember my siblings' arrival. However, I do not recall much because I was moved along to Grandmother at the time. I do remember the midwife, Mrs Suttonwood of Harwich Road, making an appearance, the pram blocking the hall and losing playing time when I had to rock the pram to get the crying infant off to sleep.

We had a large, circular, mahogany dining table and as the family grew larger, so our allotted space grew less. How strange to remember where I sat at the table; Mother at one o'clock, father at eleven o'clock without fail, and I was always at six o'clock, the others fitting in between. The twelve o' clock space was vacant because the open fireplace was there. Everyone sat down to table, grace was said and the food served in order of seniority. On the table at Mother's right hand was a small cane, and woe betide us if elbows got on to the table or any other transgression of manners occurred. Nobody left table until grace was said and that did not happen until plates were clean. Food was to be eaten, not left on the plate to be thrown away. It was all hands to clear the table afterwards. As soon as we could see over the edge of the kitchen sink we were pressed into washing-up and drying. I always tried to do the washing-up, and to this day I prefer it to drying and putting away.

The house had three bedrooms, dining/living room, kitchen and larder and, of course, the front room which was only used for special occasions. For most of my young childhood it was Great-aunt Grace's room, a sort of bed-sitter. The lavatory was part of the building but accessible only by an outside door to the left of the kitchen door. No bathroom in those days, but there was a metal bath which was kept under the kitchen table when not in use. The hot water for the bath was heated in a gas boiler in the kitchen and had to be ladled into the bath by hand. In the winter Father put the bath in front of the open fire in the living room. When we stood up for Mother to wash us from top to toe we were roasted on one side from the fire and chilled on the other by the draught from the kitchen door. Mother and Father did not have this dubious pleasure: they bathed in the kitchen with the door firmly locked. There was no central heating. Each room had an open fire but those in the bedrooms were only lit when we were ill in bed.

Greenstead in the early 1920s was like a small village on the outskirts of Colchester. There was no ribbon development as there is today. The by-pass that runs parallel to Greenstead Road had not been built and the road was the main route to London from Clacton, Walton, to a certain extent from Harwich, and for all the villages within that area. It was not tarmacked and in summer the corporation water cart would come along with its sprinkler to lay the dust. There was still a great deal of horse-drawn traffic, much of it agricultural: there were two-wheel tumbrils drawn by a single horse; four-wheel drays, lower and longer and usually drawn by two horses, and four-wheel heavy-duty wagons often pulled by four horses. Percherons, the golden-brown medium heavyweight, and the Clydesdale heavyweights were the most common breeds of horse. On Saturday mornings there would always be one and sometimes two droves of cattle, on the hoof, being taken to the market at Middleborough at the bottom of North Hill. One of my jobs was to make sure the front gate was shut to stop any cattle getting into the garden. The other was to walk into town to do the shopping for Mother.

As the ownership of cars and motorbikes increased, so summer Sundays saw the beginning of traffic jams, partly caused by the two pairs of railway gates a half-mile either side of us at the East and the Hythe, but also by the crawl through Colchester town centre. It was a favourite pastime in many a household, to watch the crawling traffic from the bedroom window. There was endless variety , open tourers, saloons with dickey seats (where the boot is on the modern car), three-wheelers, solo motorcycles, motorbikes with sidecars, bicycles, tandems and open-topped charabancs. Car makes could be picked out quite easily, with Armstrong-Siddeleys, Alvises, Clynos and Lea Francises next to the more long-lived marques of Morris, Rover and Ford. There were also the weekday workers, the steam-powered Fodens and Sentinels. I really did see the passing of horse-drawn traffic from our roads and the takeover by the internal combustion engine.

Greenstead Road never had electric trams. A service from town came down Hythe Hill to the bottom and similarly a service came down East Hill. Even when buses replaced trams, Greenstead was left out of the corporation service, but we did have Eastern National and Silver Queen buses that ran between the coast and Colchester. Until the early 1930s there was no electricity supply along Greenstead Road and we had gas lighting and later cooking. In my early years the kitchen had a built in coal-burning range, but when the gas company made suitable terms Mother invested in a gas cooker. Colchester had its own electricity-generating station in Osborne Street and eventually laid the cables to Greenstead. Special terms were offered to persuade households to be connected and we duly had the pleasure of being able to switch on. It was all strange to Mother and it took a long time to convince her that electricity could not leak like gas does.

The early electricity supply was direct current (DC) and suffered from bad regulation. This meant that if too much electricity was being used the voltage dropped and the lights dimmed. Within a few years it was changed to alternating current (AC) which was much better, and this gradually led to more electric appliances. We eventually had a mains wireless (no batteries or accumulator). I think Great-aunt Alice had a vacuum cleaner. The barber had electric hair trimmers and neon lighting made its appearance.

As with the gas, electricity was pre-paid by meter. Money had to be inserted into the meter, initially a penny, later a shilling, before power was available. It was possible to pre-pay for quite a large amount, which Mother tried to do on Father's pay day. Occasionally if a check had not been made on the meter we would be plunged into darkness because the money had run out. It was some years before I managed to persuade Mother of the economics of having a quarterly meter, and sudden loss of power were no more.

Until Mother obtained a gas boiler in the kitchen, laundry

was done in the wash-house at the back. This had a copper in one corner for heating the water, a brick-built affair that held a large copper bowl with a heavy wooden lid and a grate beneath for the fire. I learnt early on how to light the fire and used to keep the damper open on the chimney until there was a good roar. I had to report when the water was boiling, and Mother would put in the soap and soda crystals followed by the whites; when they came out, in went the coloureds. Some of the hot soapy water was then ladled into a bucket and used for scrubbing the floor. The rinsing was done in the kitchen sink with Reckitt's Blue added for the whites and Robin starch used for shirt collars and cuffs. We had a mangle with heavy wooden rollers and a large wheel at the side that had to be turned by hand to operate the rollers. The mangle was used to squeeze most of the water from the clothes, and it had an arrangement for increasing the pressure between the rollers. I did not mind mangling and used to find it fun to feed a wet soggy article — sheet, shirt or especially towels — into one side and turn the handle, watching as the water was squeezed out and the item came out the other side, flat and stiff as a board. Wash-day really was a hard day's work for mothers. Monday was always wash-day for the bulk of the family laundry, with smaller washes through the week.

Coming home from school on Mondays you would find the linoleum floors of the kitchen and dining room scrubbed and polished spotlessly clean, with newspaper laid where we would need to walk to save the floor from being soiled. In the winter the clothes horse would be open in front of the dining room fire, hung with items to dry if the weather was inclement. The horse consisted of two or three wooden frames hinged with leather strips or upholstery webbing.

These could be opened up to be free-standing, and clothes put on the rails to dry. Obviously if the clothes horse was being used the fire was obscured, so we were always pleased to see it put away.

For daily papers we had the Daily Herald at times and also the News Chronicle. I do not think this represented any particular political choice but was more the result of promotional offers. Father had the weekend magazines John Bull and Answers. They ran all sorts of competitions which he often entered but never, as far as I can remember, ever won.

It was still a simple life compared with today, but that does not imply an emptier life, far from it. Our days were full; we walked much more than today, and later on we cycled more. Family visiting was an important part of our social life.

Starting School

I do not recall starting school but I do remember those early years. Greenstead St Andrew's school, over the road from our home, had three classrooms, two at the front and the infants at the back, with its own porch and numbered hooks for our coats. The toilets were outdoors, back to back between the two playgrounds, which were separated by a high fence. The infants shared the west end playground with the girls who were strictly segregated from the senior boys.

We started school at four years old, four or five of us sitting at each long desk. These were made of pine and the seats could inflict painful splinters. Registration was conducted in silence apart from a respectful "present, Miss" from each of us, and then it was down to work.

Reading, writing and arithmetic were the main items in our work. Tables were learnt by rote, and writing by copying many times the letters written on the blackboard. We had a slate in a wooden frame and slate pencils for written work. The writing could be erased simply with a damp cloth. There was a counting frame to help us with our numbers and it had 12 horizontal wires with 12 coloured balls on each; to be called out to use the frame was the only time we left our desks during a lesson.

St Andrew's was a church school and this meant we had to know our prayers, the ten commandments and elementary bible stories, ready for the termly inspection by the Rev Clement Worsfold. Some answers we recited as a class but we lived in fear of being singled out with a question. The religious link also meant Sunday was not a free day, with Sunday school at 10 o'clock with Mr Wright the headmaster helped by Mr Hobrough, a churchwarden. At 10.45 it was up to the church for morning service at 11 o'clock, which finished about noon. Sunday school in the afternoon, 2 o'clock to 2.45, and when I was in the choir it was evening service at 6 o'clock, summer and winter. There was compensation, though: we had Ash Wednesday off after church service.

We also had regular inspections by the nit nurse, and medical and eyesight inspections, as well as occasional visits from the PE inspector. Physical education (Swedish drill) consisted of exercises standing in one place, all done in unison and to either the teacher's command or a peep on the whistle. We did not have a playing field and the only apparatus I remember was a skipping rope.

I recall a special occasion while in the infants; the year

Summer Term 1928

GREENSTEAD SCHOOL
REPORT

Name .... Ronald Rayner
Age .... 8 yrs 1 mth
Average Age in Class .... 10 yrs 4 mths
Number in Class 19
Position in Class 3rd

Points gained 200
Points lost 1
Most points gained 326
Least points lost 1

	Max.	Marks gained	Gained by top child
English	50	28	38
Reading	50	39	49
Composition	50	45	45
Poetry	50	34	45
Spelling	50	42	48
Writing	50	28	41
Arithmetic	50	32	50
Geography	50	23	30
History	50	32	38
Handwork	50	43	50
Drawing	50	34	38
Total	550	380	415

Considering Ronald's age, he has done remarkably well. He has tried hard this term to be tidier in his written work. I am very pleased with him.

R. May Tyler.
2nd Aug. 1928.

Third in class – I was two years younger than most of the other children, but I was third in class. I loved this little school, from helping Great-aunt Grace light the stoves to the slates and counting frames

must have been 1925 or 1926. We had a visit from a gentleman telling us about the League of Nations that had been created to try to stop future wars. The gentleman must have been a good speaker because he made such an impression on me that I can remember where I was sitting in the classroom.

By the age of ten I had moved through the middle room into the largest of the three rooms, which was under the control of Mr Wright the headmaster. It was a large room with the seniors at one end and the upper juniors at the other. Mr Wright had his desk on a dais and his control was complete: his cane rested by his right hand. There must have been 50 pupils in that room and yet most of the time the only sounds were the scratch of pens and the tick of the clock on the wall behind us. Mr Wright tested us on mental arithmetic and general knowledge: twenty numbers written down the side of the page and twenty questions given verbally, and a time limit set for us to give the answers.

We each in turn had to read out loud for reading lessons and we always had silent reading, which was a joy to me — Kim and the Jungle Book from Rudyard Kipling, Alice in Wonderland by Lewis Carroll, tales from Hans Christian Andersen and the Brothers Grimm ... and comics like The Rover, Adventure, The Modern Boy and the Wizard. Comics of course were at home, never in school!

Next door to the school was Mr Hillyard's tea-rooms and on summer afternoons when the classroom windows were wide open, and presumably the windows in the tea-rooms as well, one could hear the tinkle of cups and saucers and teaspoons. The sounds today still remind me of summer afternoons.

Each classroom was heated in the winter by a Tortoise

SHEET VIII.

LATERAL TRUNK MOVEMENTS. CHAP. IV.

FIG. 29.
Half Rest Half Wing Walk Outward Turn Standing Position, Trunk Bending Sideways (pages 10 and 38).

FIG. 30.
Half Wing Side Falling Position (page 39).

FIG. 31.
Feeling Breathing (hands on lower ribs). (Page 68.)

FIG. 32.
Half Wing Half Stretch Foot Grasp Half Standing, Trunk Bending Sideways (pages 20 and 39).

Swedish Drill – this was our physical education in the 1920s. There was no gymnasium or hall ... it was done in the playground.

13

coke-burning stove (incidentally first made by the Portway company some 100 years previously in Halstead, near Colchester). These stoves were placed to one side of each room near the front. As the stove was left to go out by late afternoon and not lit until an hour or two before school next day, the back part of the room was chilly in winter until mid-morning. The stove always had a bowl of water on top to stop the air getting too dry.

I had a certain kudos among my peers as Great-aunt Grace was the school caretaker, which gave me open access to the school after hours. This, though, also meant I was pressed into service to help with the Tortoise stoves. Early on I learned how to clear the ash and lay the fire ready for the morning.

The Seasons

Our young lives were governed by the seasons, far more than nowadays I think. In many ways we were luckier than youngsters of today in what we could do. How much do today's children go wandering, and how can you help with the harvest behind a combine harvester? At that time we could help load the horse and cart, and with luck were rewarded by a ride on the horse's back as it went from field to farmyard. That is no longer part of farm life.

Christmas covered several weeks, with decorations like paper chains being made both at school and at home. Carol-singing occupied several evenings and I remember going with Leslie Warboys and using my paraffin-burning cycle lamp to illuminate the hymn book and light our way. Over successive nights we covered the whole of Greenstead Road from East Gates, Miss Bryant's sweet-shop, to as far as Jacob's Hill — where the mill used to stand and now part of the Tesco superstore site. We only got pennies and ha'pennies but it enabled me to have money to spend for Christmas.

The University Boat Race, which had far more impact locally then than now, marked the end of winter. The race would occupy schoolboys' thoughts and actions for several weeks beforehand, and each and every one of us wore a light or dark blue 'favour', and defended our choice with argument — and force if need be.

We spent more time outside as the weather grew warmer and each year there would be a period when rolling hoops or spinning tops would be the dominant pastime. With lighter nights we could also explore more. The Chase, which led from Greenstead Road northwards, was well used especially by us children who lived nearby. It was a lane that led up past Berriman's farm to St Andrew's church, opposite which was a kissing gate to the five-field walk to Bromley Road and Parson's Heath. A footpath also went off to the right to Hythe Station Road. The Chase continued past the church until it reached Park Farm and a huge manure heap, after which it veered to the right and descended past Coppens farmhouse to Salary Brook and on to Hearts Hill. From the base of the hill it became a footpath which went over the hill and either through Churnwood to Crockleford, or right to the lane over the Clacton road through Wivenhoe Park — a way back home if we wished. Where The Chase crossed Salary Brook the stream widened and deepened into a pool and it was a favourite spot for attempts at swimming. Rarely was anything planned. If we were going that way and the sun was high then we just stripped and had a dip, drying in the sun. Enjoying ourselves one afternoon we were concerned to see the choirmistress Miss Stammers, a prim and proper lady, approaching us. Down we went into the pool to save both her — and our — embarrassment, expecting her to walk quickly past. To our dismay she stopped to tell us about a choir practice that we must attend. What a relief when she and her dog moved on.

Summer was harvest time: peas to be picked at Mr Berriman's farm, earning us 1s 6d for a large sack; following the reaping machine and stacking the sheaves into stooks, hoping to catch a rabbit that might dash out, and picking gooseberries at Uncle Arthur's market garden and salvaging windfall apples to sell at his shop.

In summer the Army was out on manoeuvres from the town's large garrison. Four abreast the soldiers would march, the band playing and the field kitchen bringing up the rear. I was allowed to follow them as far as Jacob's Hill. Those same soldiers would provide the spectacle of church parade on Sundays opposite the Garrison church. In fine weather, Father would walk us up to watch this parade while Mother prepared dinner. We thought nothing of the walk of at least three miles — Greenstead Road, East Street, Brook Street, Wimpole Road and Military Road. If it was hot, we looked forward to the lemonade that Father would buy us in Went's shop in East Street on the way home.

Late summer and there were blackberries along The Chase and past St Andrew's church, all now part of the Greenstead estate. Our school caps were useful containers. Outward bound we had a good feast; if we picked as we wended our way home then Mother made use of the berries for an apple and blackberry pie — my favourite — or a pudding, which was father's choice. Summertime also gave me the opportunity of joining Uncle Arthur in his farm delivery business. He owned a late Model 'T' Ford truck and did work for Marriage's at East Mill. We would load up sacks of feed, poultry pellets, Ovum, a supplement for chickens that had a lovely spicy smell about it, and anything else that farmers would be using. My job was to jump up on the back and move the sacks to the edge so Uncle Arthur could then carry them on his shoulders to the barn or whatever. I cannot imagine that a ten or 11-year-old would be allowed anywhere near the back of a truck nowadays. I enjoyed it and managed to visit a great number of the farms within 20 miles of Colchester. I remember one trip to Maldon: we had to go up the hill and, as we were well loaded, I had to jump out at the bottom and go round to the back and push. We made it. Those old Ford trucks were spartan and the rear of the engine protruded into the cabin. The flywheel was also part of the ignition system and the flywheel cover had some terminals on it. If you inadvertently touched one with a nail in your shoe or boot, the shock woke you up.

Autumn was the time for conkers and sweet chestnuts. The school playground had several horse chestnut trees but the sweet chestnuts we collected in great numbers from Wivenhoe Park. The landowner Mr Gooch and his keepers did not look too kindly on us wandering from the footpath. Avoiding confrontation while still gathering chestnuts added to the pleasure of the expedition. In the early 1930s a lot of roadworks were being carried out as the first Colchester bypass was built from Greenstead Road to Lexden and the contractors always had a night-watchman. He had a little hut and a coke-burning brazier and we would persuade him to place our sweet chestnuts on a shovel over the glowing fire. They have never tasted so good! Guy Fawkes' Night was another marker in the year, and the build-up to the Fifth of November usually saw bangers let off in the school playground by some of the seniors.

Late autumn and winter curtailed our activities but the threshing provided some excitement. The harvest of wheat, oats and barley had been stored after reaping. When work on the fields eased so the threshing tackle was set up, driven by a steam engine. As the men worked down through the sheaves to feed the threshing drum, so rats would leap and run. Our excitement came from chasing the vermin with as big a stick as we could handle in a vain attempt to kill them.

Darker nights meant we were outside less but one winter evening sticks out in my mind. Father had been to the coalhouse to fill the scuttle then took me out into the back yard. We witnessed a remarkable display in the sky: the Aurora Borealis or Northern Lights. The evening was clear and cold, and the sky fascinating and beautiful.

Seaside Fun

A wonderful part of our family life was our visits to the seaside, mostly made by train from the Hythe station, usually on Sundays because Father would be working on Saturday mornings. If the weather looked promising on Saturday then preparations were made for an early start the next day. We would get hats and buckets and spades ready by the evening and Mother would rise early on the Sunday to prepare the picnic.

The trains to Clacton and Walton on summer Sundays were busy and we would wait impatiently by the front gate, anxious to be on our way and noting all the other families on their way to the station. We agonised over missing the train — we never did.

The ticket office was on the London-bound or 'up' side and I always tried to go in with Father to buy the tickets. Mr Hubbard was the stationmaster and he was often behind the hatch and seemed to know Father because he greeted him by name. On the wall behind Mr Hubbard I could see the telegraphs and hear their click-clacking as messages were passed along the line. A confirmation that tickets were bought was the thump as the date was stamped on each one. It was no feeble hand-stamp but a solid cast-iron pedestal with a foot pedal.

We had to cross the lines to the other platform and it felt a daring thing to do. The gates would be closed to traffic and as we crossed the tracks we could look to right and left along the lines. The platform would be crowded. As the steam-hauled train approached, the porters would shout for everyone to stand back. What jostling followed was good-natured as families struggled to keep together, there were no corridors on the local trains.

Trains from the Hythe would carry seaside-bound passengers as far as Thorpe. They then split in two with one half going on to Clacton and the other to Walton. This would cause Mother considerable anxiety in case we were on the Walton half and only had tickets for Clacton, or vice-versa. We were relieved when we realised all was well, particularly Father who bore the responsibility at the Hythe for selecting the correct part of the train.

Usually we went to Walton for, as Mother said, "the sand

was much better" and there was more of it, and the place itself was not as noisy. Looking back I realise Mother did not appreciate the crowds of Londoners, obviously East Enders, for whom Clacton was a favourite.

Mother saw Walton as a little more genteel. We, the children, were not concerned with such matters. Suffice that the sun, sand and sea were ours to enjoy for a whole day, while Father and Mother relaxed on their deckchairs with the sandwiches and drinks placed in the shade behind them to keep them cool.

The paddle steamers carrying people from London and the Thames-side towns were regular visitors to the pier and, as they passed by, we would be warned to watch out for the wave from their wash. Children had been knocked over by them as they paddled, or so we were told.

Late afternoon would see us walking back to the station. The railway carriage would be too hot and Mother would plead for the window to be lowered, the need for fresh air to be balanced against the discomfort from the smoke and smuts blown in from the engine.

For me the fitting end to a wonderful day was the stretch of line from Wivenhoe to the Hythe that ran alongside the River Colne. If the tide was flooding, there would be two, three or four sailing barges making their stately way up to the Hythe. What a wonderful sight it was.

Were summers warmer and more settled or do simple pleasures leave deeper memories? Little wonder my generation is nostalgic about steam trains: the smell of smoke and steam; the calls of the porter as he walked the length of the platform slamming shut the doors, and the scramble to get a window seat, especially one facing forward.

If you were lucky you could look at the paintings on the

compartment walls of places the railways visited — Skegness, Bournemouth, Edinburgh, Llandudno — the ends of the earth to us in our small world.

Wireless wonder

To begin with, we had no radio, or wireless as it was called, but always books and family games such as ludo, tiddlywinks, snakes and ladders, lotto, dominoes and simple playing-card games. As we got older, cribbage was introduced as it was one of Father's favourites. One year a relative gave me a toy gramophone that played six-inch sized records (6d from Woolworths) and I think this led Mother and Father to buy a proper gramophone that gave us tremendous entertainment. I'm sure it also helped Father because he had a good singing voice and used to perform at "smoking concerts".

Our first wireless was a gift from Great-aunt Alice. It had a mahogany cabinet about the size of a small television, with knobs and switches on the front. In among the works were two or three glass valves, two coils that could be moved nearer to or away from each other, and a device for tuning in a station and a smaller one for what was called "reaction". I later learnt that these were moveable condensers. The loudspeaker was a large horn in the form of a question mark set on a heavy metal base about six inches in diameter.

The power came from a number of small batteries in a cardboard container held together by pitch, and from an accumulator. This accumulator, a smaller version of those used in cars, made the valves in the wireless light up. After

The Hythe, Colchester – there was always something to see
Postcards courtesy of camulos.com

several hours, the wireless would lose power and the accumulator had to be disconnected and taken over the road to Mr Keeling's garage to be recharged. We had two accumulators, one was in use while the other was on charge. Our aerial was fixed to a tall pole at the end of the garden, with the wire fixed to the top via a porcelain insulator. The other end of the wire led to the wireless via an insulator fixed beneath the guttering and then down to the windowsill.

Modern television is a remarkable achievement but it did not have the same impact as that first wireless. We went from tapping our feet to a wind-up gramophone to listening to speech or music coming from London — with no visible connection. If conditions were right we could even hear foreigners. It was more than a transformation: it was a miracle!

In second or third year science lessons at secondary school, I made my own home-made radio — a crystal set — that worked without batteries and used headphones. It fitted in a cigar-box and could be used at bedtime when reception was always much better. I was often lulled to sleep by late-night dance music from one of the leading London hotels with bands such as Ray Noble, Lew Stone or Geraldo.

Hythe adventures

As soon as Mother let me roam farther than the immediate neighbourhood, I began to spend happy hours along the river watching the barges and coasters. The Hythe was a busy place with the railway extending down both sides of the river, particularly the south side where it went as far as the electricity generating station, well beyond Distillery Lane. At the generating station coal trucks were shunted into a steel frame one by one. They were tipped upside down and the coal dropped on to an underground conveyor belt. It was well worth watching so long as you stood upwind to avoid the black dust.

Almost opposite on the other river bank was the Moler brick works. Its large overhead crane unloaded the mainly Dutch boats bringing a special type of earth from Denmark. The Moler made both fireproof bricks and insulation bricks and they were light enough to float for a while. The Dutch boats always seemed so clean. The crew, who wore clogs on deck, stepped out of them before entering the living quarters.

Other regular boats were the colliers from the North-East bringing coal for the gasworks. Many of them belonged to a company called Everard and all their names ended in "ity" — Audacity, Alacrity and so on. When turning to leave, they were high in the water because they had no cargo. They sometimes had problems in the swinging berth; if a strong wind was blowing directly up or down the river, their manoeuvring was entertaining.

Beyond the gasworks towards Hythe bridge were the Pauls' oil and feed mills. Occasionally, much to our delight, a barge would arrive with a load of peanuts, but mostly the cargo was linseed. One could stand by the open door and watch the linseed being pressed for the oil. The residue came out like a flat board and became animal feed. The barrels would be stacked outside, but sometimes the oil was collected by a dirty old tanker called the Broiler.

The sailing barges were my greatest interest and I can remember seeing barges lined up bow to stern along both sides of the river from the bridge down to the bend at the swinging berth. Many were destined for Marriage's Mill at East Bay and to get there they had to lower masts and sails to be able to take the tide under the bridges — the road bridges at the Hythe and East Street, and three railway bridges. The barges were moved by the crew pushing on poles much like you propel a punt. The crew would move to the bow, drop one end of the pole to the riverbed and, with the other end pressed to their shoulder, walk towards the stern and propel the barge forward. Apart from grain I recall seeing cargoes of timber and cement for Groom Daniels, and tarred roadstone for Essex County Council, which had its own crane and yard. There was also hay and straw stacked high ready to be taken up the Thames to London.

Near to Hythe bridge fronting Hawkins Road was the canning factory — vegetables in summer, fish in winter. Beside it was another granary and elevator, and two on the other side farther down. This granary next to the canning factory always had a small heap of sweepings smouldering away outside the elevator, and we were able to pick up maize and turn it into popcorn in the hot ashes.

Just off the riverside up Distillery Lane was Distillery Pond and the Albany Laundry. If we were cold we could stand on the higher ground by the laundry's open windows to enjoy the steamy air. The pond itself was great fun: in winter, if conditions were right, it was used for ice-skating.

Downriver beyond the generating station was Clift's sawmill where home-grown timber became usable material. We often saw the steam traction engine pulling a load of tree trunks along Greenstead Road on the way to the mill. At the sawmill we would stand outside the fence to watch the sawyers at work.

Past the sawmill were the maltings and we could watch the maltsters turn the sprouting barley on the wooden floor. We always appreciated the nutty aroma, which was more than could be said for the smells from the Whambacks and the Haven Road knackers' yard where animal carcasses and bones were rendered.

The road parallel to the river finished at the council sewage works. At the entrance to the works was an engine house with a large engine, which I think was steam-powered. It had a huge flywheel half-sunk in the floor. It was fascinating to watch this gleaming monster, with brass work polished and bare metal oiled and shining. It must have been a pumping station because next to it was a large metal grid. You could stand on it and see underneath what was presumably the sewage flowing from the town.

The last interesting feature was beyond the sewage works on the river's edge. It was the bucket elevator where the barges full of mud from the dredger were emptied. The dredger worked the tides to clear mud from the riverbed. It had an endless chain of steel buckets that were lowered to the riverbed where they scooped up mud. As they came up the other side, the buckets were tilted and the mud emptied into a barge tied alongside. The barges were towed downstream and the mud deposited in lagoons where it dried out.

High tide or low there was always something of interest going on along the river between Hythe bridge and the sewage outfall. It is sad to look at it today and to remember what an area of trading activity it once was.

Sickness Strikes

I never left junior school in the sense of walking out of the gate on the last day. The Christmas before the summer of 1930, I was with the family with Uncle Harry and Aunt Eva, Jimmy and Dinah, who lived four doors along Greenstead Road. On Boxing Day evening I felt poorly with a sore throat and headache. Next day Dr Hickinbotham was called and I was rushed in to the Isolation Hospital at Myland, now demolished, although the water tower remains on Mill Road.

Diphtheria was a serious illness with a high chance of dying. I did not know that, though I was aware of the concern of the nurses and matron, who placed some sort of restriction round my bed to keep contact between the nurses, other patients and me to a minimum.

What a trial it must have been for Mother and Father. To get there meant a bus ride to the town centre and then another bus to the hospital. When they got there, they faced two hours standing outside my window looking in with just a small veranda to protect them from the weather.

This they had to do through January, February and March before the weather eased at all. Any goodies they brought had to be handed to reception and the nurse would bring them to me. I particularly remember that eggs, as extras to our meals, had to have your name written on them so they went to the right patient. Mr Purser our milkman was an occasional visitor as he had a relative in the hospital at the same time. He brought me eggs, too.

Life in hospital was regimented and matron's morning inspection was rigorous. Beds were made with sheets turned down so they were in a straight line from one end of the ward to the other. You couldn't have comics, books or toys on display, and locker tops had to be clear. Matron was a person of authority but I have no unhappy memories of my stay, apart from missing family and school friends.

My primary school headmistress, Miss Glynn, was concerned about me as one of her brighter pupils. She helped to get me into the Passmore Edwards Convalescent Home for a month after I left hospital.

The home was situated towards Holland-on-Sea, about 18 miles from Colchester. It is near the seafront, but the made-up road that now runs from Clacton to Holland stopped short before it reached Passmore Edwards, leaving a rough track next to the grassed clifftop. I remember hot sunny days, paddling and bathing, picnics in a nearby meadow and 'falling in love' with a girl from the Southend area by the name of Iris Patten. I wonder if Iris ever thought of me after we went our separate ways? The school summer term was almost over by the time I was home for good. It was then I found out that when I had been taken to hospital all the family were medically examined and the house fumigated. Luckily no-one else developed the illness.

I had a further six weeks before school in September. Diphtheria put paid to my hopes of getting to the boys' grammar school and it is tempting to speculate how different my life would have been if I had not fallen ill.

My First Bike

At the age of 11 I bought my first bicycle. It cost just over £3, which was a week's wages for many. Mother paid for it and I paid her back weekly from my earnings — I did a milk round for Mr Purser. Having the bike meant I could go farther afield exploring. One of our usual summer trips was to Brightlingsea for a swim in the newly-opened pool, sometimes at weekends, sometimes in the evening. There were usually several of us — boys only of course — and we covered an area from West Mersea to Harwich in our cycling expeditions, on much quieter roads than we have today.

When I was about nine or ten, Mother had arranged for me to go and stay with Aunt Louie for a few days. I was going to be put on the train at the Hythe Station in the care of the guard and Aunt Louie was to meet me at Liverpool Street Station. Everything was organised, my bag packed and then the day before I was due to go I went down with mumps. I never did get that holiday. Looking back one realises how trusting people were. I do not think such travel arrangements would be countenanced today.

Aircraft Overhead

On a Sunday morning in early May 1926 we all went outside to watch the Italian airship Norge fly over Colchester. It was heading for the North Pole which it overflew on May 12. This was a very special event, distinguished from the special events of aeroplanes flying over our home. Aircraft were few and far between and always occasioned a dash outside to watch them.

By the early 1930s there were more aeroplanes, including Sir Alan Cobham's Flying Circus, which paid a visit to Colchester. They flew from Blue Barns aerodrome, a large field beside the old Ipswich Road near Ardleigh. I remember cycling there and being allowed to touch one of the planes. Oh, the fascination and wonderment of watching them take off and land, and do daredevil acrobatic stunts.

Little did we realise in those innocent days the impact that aeroplanes were to have on our lives within a few short years.

Pocket Money

We had no pocket money as it is given today. Sometimes we were given a few pennies for a special task in the home but that was a rare event — Mother had little to spare, goodness knows. Most coins we had were earned by running errands for other people, fruit picking, weeding gardens, sweeping snow or collecting horse-manure for Uncle Sam to use on his allotment. As well as my bicycle milk round I delivered hot meat pies for the couple next door: Mr Tomlinson had been laid off work, his wife was a good cook and so they started a business making and selling meat pies. I used Mr Tomlinson's trade cycle for that job and I regularly had coins in my pocket. With Mother's encouragement I spent some of my largesse on a seven-volume encyclopaedia, bought on subscription. Were we hard done by? We never thought so. We enjoyed life however it came and never had time to be bored.

Scouting and Sailing

From Cub to Rover Scout I enjoyed 13 years of deep friendships, sharing adventures and lessons in leadership for which I am forever grateful.

In 1926 I joined the Cubs, being allowed in by Miss Laurie as a special favour. The starting age then was eight and I was only seven. That was the beginning of Scouting which, over many years, gave me tremendous pleasure, support and guidance. The troop was the 12th Colchester and we met on Fridays in the Congregational Chapel, Harwich Road, near to the railway crossing (I'm told that the Cubs only stopped using that hall in 2005, when it was pulled down).

Whitsun of 1926 and I went to my first camp, at Great Horkesley, about four miles from home. We slept in bell tents, feet to the tent pole and head to the circular wall of the tent. There were no sleeping bags and instead we had palliasses that we filled with straw to make mattresses, and blankets that we pinned with blanket pins to make our beds. The pins were about four inches long and I still have mine. We had a thunderstorm on the first night: the next day Mother made Father cycle over to see if I was all right; I was, and thoroughly enjoying myself. Many camps followed this but none was as exciting as the first. In the early to mid 1930s, Maurice Bond (newly retired from the sea) joined Jack Russell and Don Scott in running the troop. Under Maurice's guidance a Sea Scouts section was started which I enthusiastically joined. We obtained an ex-naval whaler complete with sails and sweeps and a clinker 14ft pulling dinghy, but we needed to make a base at West Mersea. One of our members was Gordon Flory whose family owned a building company, and he found that the Army was getting rid of wooden huts from Colchester barracks. We obtained one which we dismantled and took to Mersea. With Gordon's firm's help and our own labour we managed it, and the hut was erected in City Lane on a plot of land given by a lady whose name, regretfully, I cannot recall. The Sea Scouts' fleet of boats was later increased to three by the addition of an 18ft clinker-built fixed-keel Bermudan sloop, a real beauty to sail.

Three years of sailing followed, which I count as three of the most enjoyable years of my early life. We sailed round to Woolverstone on the River Orwell for summer camp, having gained permission to pitch our tents in the grounds of Woolverstone School, then administered by London County Council. The boats were moored in the river just below us.

On one occasion, the 18-footer had to be left behind until the next weekend. Maurice and I agreed to bring it back, so early the next Sunday we were driven over to catch the tide. I was glad it was a morning job as I had a date with a nice young lady that evening. It was warm and sunny, and we made good progress downriver. By the time we reached the Naze, however, the breeze was faltering, and we were eventually becalmed off Clacton. There was no engine, so there we stayed, lolloping about with the slight swell and using the long sweep to keep us heading the right way. We picked up our mooring in West Mersea several hours late — and all hope of meeting the young lady was dashed. A budding romance had been blown away by a fickle breeze and, to the best of my knowledge, that young lady never married.

On summer weekends three of us would take the 18-footer, often to explore the River Blackwater. We had a canvas cover that went over the boom and was tied to the deck to make it like a tent, and we slept on the bottom boards. Cooking was done on a Primus stove. Day sailing would often be across to Bradwell — there was no marina then, but a welcoming pub — or up to Ray Island for a picnic and swimming.

One of the highlights of this time was a trip to Discovery, Scott of Antarctica's ship moored on the Thames embankment. We were shown around the ship, had a meal in the ward room, let loose to explore the decks and to get the feel of the vessel, then lived aboard for the weekend. Sleeping in one of the bunks was a great experience, pondering on which member of the expedition had slept there before me. We rowed one of the ship's boats up the Thames and were quite surprised at the force of the tide.

On Christmas morning we used to help at the Corn Exchange in Colchester, where a Christmas breakfast was provided for the less well-off residents of the town. It was always a festive occasion and a good way to start the day.

In the 1930s, Ralph Reader and the Scout Association had great success in London's West End with their Gang Shows, which were musical revues with an all-Scouts cast that played to packed theatres. Colchester and District Scout Association decided to follow the idea, and in the 1938-39 shows, I was a willing and eager performer, but

Gang Show laughs in 1938-39. I am the ballerina, far left.

never a major star. The Colchester shows were held in the Albert Hall in the High Street, where the Co-op Bank is now. According to the 1939 programme EH Skinner was the producer, Tom Hammond musical director, and the show ran for ten nights with a matinee on Easter Monday. In the 1938 show the grand finale was a ballet danced to Mendelssohn's Spring Song. There were ten of us: our principal Len Bridges, two sub-principals and seven supporting dancers. We were dressed in frilly skirts , proper dancing shoes and wigs; mine was blonde. With much practice we reached a reasonable standard of movement but ballerinas we were not. The sight of ten gangly teenagers trying to be serious dancers must have been incongruous to say the least. I know we all enjoyed it — and so did the audience for each performance prompted lots of laughter and applause. As one critic declared: "The act brought the house down". It is the nearest I shall ever be to fame on the stage.

I have already mentioned my Scout leaders including dear Miss Laurie. There were many members of Colchester and District Scouts whose company and support I was privileged to enjoy. They included David Papillon who donated the camp at Thorrington which we helped to clear and set up, Scout shop owner Hugh Markham, and the newspaperman Hervey Benham, who often took us out on his smack and sometimes for a bit of fishing which provided a good meal when the anchor was dropped.

One of the activities that was part of the Scouting scene, although not strictly Scouting, was the hiking club. Organised by Mr Rowland it was open to all the troops in the area for members over 16. Hikes took place on winter Sundays and warm clothes and waterproof shoes were essential. Each hike had a place of interest to visit and I remember

Layer Marney Tower, the sugarbeet factory at Ipswich, and what was then the Xylonite works at Brantham where we watched men making the plastic bodies of bicycle pumps. The process involved flammable materials and we had to leave outside anything metal in case a spark was produced.

Another sideline to Scouting was the gym club run by one of the Dowman brothers on Monday evenings. It was held in the old Bunting Room gym in Culver Street, near Bank Passage. It was strenuous activity but we enjoyed it. Afterwards we would gather at the Milk Bar in St John's Street, opposite the bus park that used to be there. It was quite a meeting place for young people.

In retrospect, I realise how different life was for young people in the days before the war. We were free to take risks and we were far less affluent: money had to be earned and carefully spent. Sex was not the dominant factor it is today. It was there, but easy contraception was not. Make no mistake, passion and ardour were present but our desires were tempered by worries of illegitimacy and bastardy. Shame was a heavy burden. Wonderful years, wonderful friends. The second world war was to end some of those friendships as some pals never returned. I was lucky.

Senior School

Having missed any chance of going to the boys' grammar school, I was sent to Hamilton Road school. In the 1930s this was a second-string grammar school. After the initial trauma of moving to a large school on the other side of town from a church school on my doorstep, 1930 to 1934 proved to be happy years. Hamilton Road was a mixed school with roughly equal numbers of boys and girls, although the playgrounds were segregated and the respective cloakrooms and toilets were at opposite ends of the building.

Mr Reeve was headmaster and he was strict but fair and likeable. He was fond of quoting the proverb "Procrastination is the thief of time" if he came across any of us showing signs of what he considered a major sin — the wasting of time in any form or fashion.

Other names that come to mind are Mrs Hobday, senior mistress; Mr Soar for art; Miss Clarke for French; Miss Parker for English; Mr Botterill for science; Mr Steele for handicraft; Mr Rudsdale for mathematics; Mr Sutton for commerce, and Miss Harris for geography. We started on a common syllabus and then divided into either technical or commercial syllabuses. The technical syllabus had more geometry and mensuration in the mathematics teaching, more science/physics and more woodwork/metalwork. The commercial syllabus had book-keeping, shorthand and typing, and domestic science.

There were no school meals but those of us who came from a fair distance could take sandwiches and eat them in the domestic science room. The mid-day break was fairly long to enable pupils and staff to go home if they wished, and in the better weather I often cycled to have dinner with the family. My route was Butt Road, St John's Street, Vineyard Street, Priory Street, East Hill, East Gates and Greenstead Road. It was possible to catch a Corporation bus by walking either to East Gates or the bottom of Hythe Hill and then getting one along Maldon Road or Butt Road. There was a time when we had some assistance for bus travel. I think we were given a number of unpunched tickets to use at our

Pupil's Name Ronald Rayner

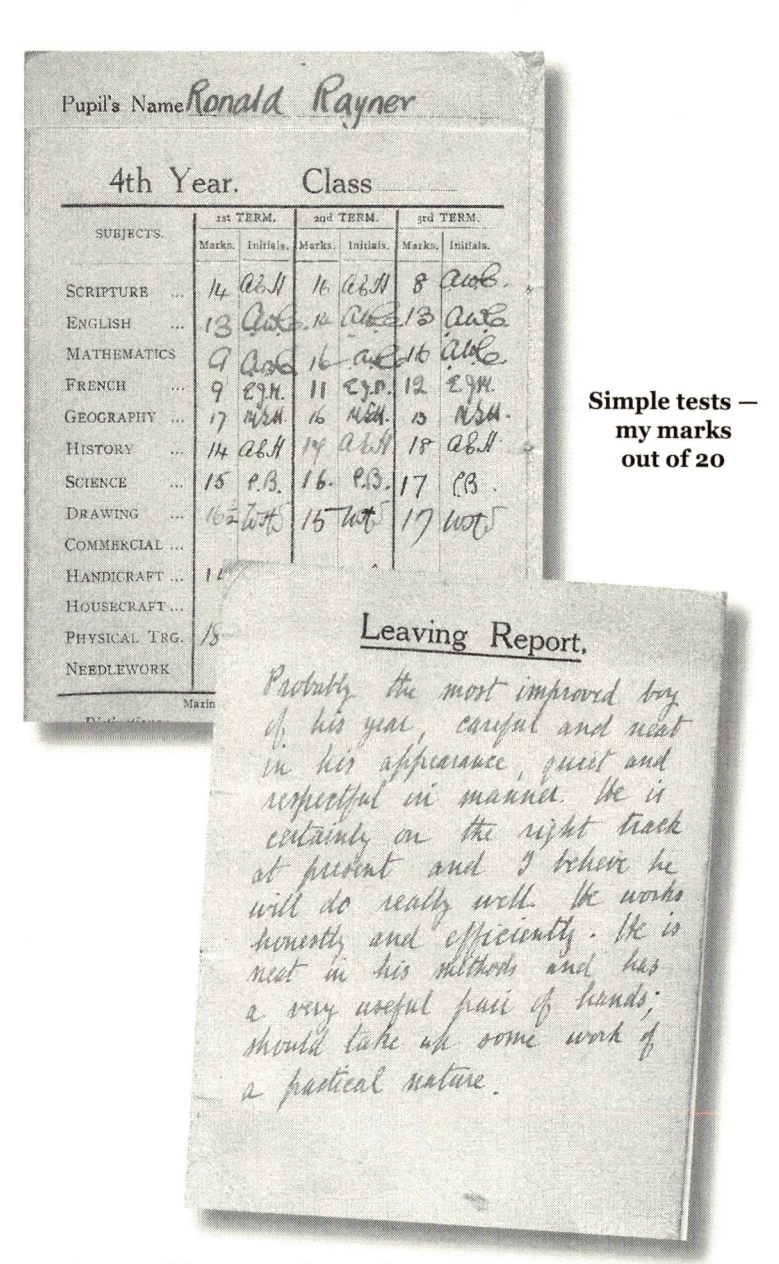

4th Year. Class

SUBJECTS	1st TERM Marks	1st TERM Initials	2nd TERM Marks	2nd TERM Initials	3rd TERM Marks	3rd TERM Initials
SCRIPTURE	14	A&H	16	A&H	8	A&B
ENGLISH	13	A&B	12	A&B	13	A&B
MATHEMATICS	9	A&B	16	A&B	16	A&B
FRENCH	9	E.J.H.	11	E.J.P.	12	E.J.H.
GEOGRAPHY	17	N.J.M.	16	N.J.M.	15	N.J.M.
HISTORY	14	A&H	17	A&H	18	A&H
SCIENCE	15	P.B.	16	P.B.	17	P.B.
DRAWING	16½	W.J.S	15	W.J.S	17	W.J.S
COMMERCIAL						
HANDICRAFT	12					
HOUSECRAFT						
PHYSICAL TRG.	15					
NEEDLEWORK						

Simple tests — my marks out of 20

Leaving Report.

Probably the most improved boy of his year, careful and neat in his appearance, quiet and respectful in manner. He is certainly on the right track at present and I believe he will do really well. He works honestly and efficiently. He is neat in his methods and has a very useful pair of hands; should take up some work of a practical nature.

Great strides – I made good progress at Hamilton Road school, but I still remember a teacher's gift of a comb

convenience. Caning or the slipper was the punishment for major indiscipline. Minor faults, usually relating to homework either badly done or not done at all, resulted in time spent 'under the clock'. The upper floor corridor ran from one end of the block to the other with classrooms off to each side; halfway along the corridor the school clock hung on the wall. Miscreants had to stand under this clock and suffer the humiliation of being seen by most of the school at lesson change-overs. I still remember how I felt when I suffered the punishment. It was certainly a deterrent. The writing of lines was also a common punishment, the severity of your offence reflected by the number of lines, rarely below one hundred, with the content dictated by the teacher. "I must remember to hand in my homework at the correct time" was a fairly regular item. There were no Biros then: our pens were a holder with a replaceable nib, and you dipped the nib into the inkwell to pick up enough ink for a line of writing. We soon perfected a method of using two pens held together by elastic bands so that two lines could be written at the same time. It did require an ink container with a wide opening to dip in the nibs. We all aspired to have a fountain pen as they held a good supply of ink. Pupils who had these filled them by placing the nib in the ink and pumping a little lever on the side of the pen barrel until the rubber tube inside was full of ink.

At the end of term at Christmas there was a full assembly in the school hall with carols, and there was also a Christmas tree with presents. We hoped we were not to be favoured with these as the "presents" were intended to impress upon the recipient a need to mend his or her ways in some way. During my second year I received a hair comb and I have never forgotten the lesson it was meant to convey! It was all good fun and drove home the intended message. School leaving age was 14 but at Hamilton Road we did an extra year so I left school in July 1934. Further full-time education was neither widespread nor easily obtainable and certainly the family budget could not offer any help. So it was that I found myself on a labour market suffering from a deep economic depression. With more than two million unemployed in a labour force far smaller than that of today, the prospect was not bright and there was no social security or welfare handouts of any kind.

Fortunately, Father was in charge of the process for producing cast-iron at FW Brackett's foundry. He came home one day in late autumn to tell me of a vacancy in the pattern-shop and so I began work.

World of Work

FW Brackett was a general engineering company and foundry with an emphasis on water-screening equipment for power stations. The work was varied and interesting. My apprenticeship as an engineering pattern-maker started in the autumn of 1934. My hours of work were Monday to Friday 8am to 5.30pm and Saturday 8am to 12.30pm. There were five men and the foreman, Charles Nunn, in the pattern-shop with me, the junior apprentice. My bench was farthest from the heating stove and winter mornings were a trial until about 11am when the place had warmed up.

We had a store-keeper, Harry, who brewed up our morning cup of tea, kept the stove going and swept the place clean. He was a veteran of the Great War and had suffered in one of the poison gas episodes. A great teller of tales he regaled us with his experiences whenever the foreman was out of the shop. The lorry driver, Billy Rand, would call in occasionally and he also had served in the 1914-1918 war. I still remember listening as a sixteen-year-old to him recounting the first time he visited a brothel in France. He told how he was accosted on the stairs by a luscious naked woman. It was too much for a sex-starved young man and matters reached their climax before he could accomplish anything. As he said: "What was worse, wasted effort or wasted money?"

Pattern-making was the step in between the drawings being produced in the drawing office and the casting being made in the foundry. If an object had to be cast in metal, a replica had to be produced, usually in wood, by working from the draughtsman's drawings. Special allowances were made for the interior of the object and for the contraction of the metal as it cooled after casting. The wooden pattern was used to make a mould in sand, and the molten metal poured into the mould. Brackett's had its own foundry for cast-iron but contracted out work in brass, bronze, aluminium and stainless steel. The foundry was situated roughly where the entrance road to Greenstead Tesco superstore is now. The drawing office fronted Hythe Station Road and the pattern-shop was midway between. Consultation was sometimes necessary particularly with the foundry, sometimes with the drawing office and occasionally with the machine shop, and these visits broadened my experience and were a great help to me during subsequent City and Guilds exams that I took at the Technical College on North Hill, now Colchester Sixth Form College, to supplement my apprenticeship.

Brackett's also produced pumps of various sizes, both for liquids and for vacuum, food processing and canning machinery and, rarely in my early years, stationary steam engines.

When the Avenue of Remembrance was created on Colchester by-pass, each tree on Cymbeline Way was given a cast plate attached to the cage protecting the sapling. These plates recorded the details of the donor and the person or persons being remembered. Some of the wording was standard and a basic plate was used as a pattern with new letters being stuck on for each message. That was a job that often came my way! The new plate was cast in aluminium at the foundry at the nearby village of Copford. I still have the list of the donors and sponsors of those trees.

We also did work for the Colchester Lathe Company which was situated between Brackett's and the railway line. That was always an interesting visit when a problem had to be solved.

To make sure we were at work the company had us clock-on and clock-off each day. Everyone had a clock number, mine was 9, and in a rack next to the clock was a numbered card for each worker. The clock telling the time was inside a large circular ring with numbered holes around it corresponding to the number of cards in the rack. To clock on or off you moved an arm round to your number after putting your card in a slot. By pushing down on the arm the time was printed on the card. If you clocked-on three minutes late you lost a quarter of an hour's time deducted from your wage. My weekly wage when I started in 1934 was 7s 3d (37½p). When I left in 1939 my wage had increased to 27s 6d (£1.37 ½p).

Finishing work was dictated by the works' hooter. The

three engineering firms in the area, Brackett's, the Lathe Company and Paxman's, each had their own hooter and there was rarely any synchronisation.

Conditions at Brackett's compared favourably with those generally accepted at the time. There was no works canteen and it was either walking or cycling home for dinner or taking a packed lunch. Neither was there a morning or afternoon tea break, but they came in eventually. Toilets were adequate but spartan — there was no hot water and certainly no showers.

Life was going well but there were clouds on the horizon. Hitler and the Nazis were creating problems in Europe and in 1938 our government introduced a form of conscription. There were limited choices for us as we turned 19: training in the Army, Navy or RAF, or coal-mining. I would dearly have loved the Navy but wiser counsel prevailed; my peers knew how seasickness could distress and demoralise me. I joined the Royal Air Force Volunteer Reserve as No 753004 and trained week-ends at the seaplane base at Felixstowe.

We did not do any square-bashing – the hours of marching drill that new recruits normally undergo – but instead had training in the maintenance of planes such as the Swordfish and the Gladiator, the so-called stringbags in which rigging and trim were so important.

One day in late August 1939 I was called from work to meet Mother at the main works gate. Greatly distressed she told me she had just heard on the wireless that there was a general call-up and as a reservist I had to report to the RAF depot in Ipswich. That was the last day of work at F W Brackett's for almost six years.

This picture of me was taken by a Colchester photographer. Mother had it included in an exhibition of pictures of the town's young people joining the services, which was staged in the gas company shop in Head Street

Fighting Hitler

At Ipswich, the RAF did not really know what to do with us and certainly it did not have enough uniforms for us all. For six weeks we had to report to Ipswich and then wait at home for further orders. Eventually I was posted to a barrage balloon depot at Alvaston, Derbyshire, with a fellow called Knights from Felixstowe, both of us classed as carpenters as that was the only RAF classification into which we could be fitted.

We arrived at the unit late evening and had to be on parade at 8am the next day. We were still short of items of uniform and we both turned up minus a hat. The warrant officer nearly had a fit but, after we explained, all was well. Because of my scouting experiences in sharing accommodation, I did not find the transition to service life too difficult. The huts at the barracks were fairly new and well appointed with adequate toilet and washing facilities, laundry room and heating. We were put on a rota to be the room orderly. This job meant ensuring the room was spotless, ready for inspection by the Commanding Officer at 10am daily. The way that this chore was shared quickly exposed those who were inadequate, lazy or indifferent, much to the consternation of the rest of us. Failure to pass inspection meant sanctions against everyone. Barrack room justice can be effective, and the back-sliders were soon pulling their weight and keen to prove their worth.

We had one member who persisted in going out drinking. He returned after lights out, disturbing us with his noise and erratic behaviour. He quickly learned his lesson. As soon as his snoring signalled that he was asleep, a bucket of water was placed by his bed and one of his hands gently immersed, which invariably caused him to wet his bed.

The chat and gossip in the 10 or 15 minutes after lights out was most entertaining. Sex tended to be a regular topic and some of the tales of seduction, frequency and stamina, if true, broadened my mind and made me wonder about my own capabilities. One fellow, about my age, boasted that he could knock eight half-crowns in line off the tabletop with his erect member. We never saw it proved. Nobody was prepared to lose that much money.

The unit was the servicing base for the balloon barrage placed around Derby, mainly to protect the Rolls-Royce engine works. We did not have a lot to do — there is not much in the way of woodwork on a barrage balloon! However, the establishment of the place listed two carpenters and so there we were. Life was fairly easy, we had quite a lot of free time but obviously I did miss home. The winter of 1939-40 saw us on night-time patrol around the depot perimeter because of terrorist threats. What we could have done I do not know. We had no guns and made do with pick-axe handles. During that winter and spring I was involved with the first-aid unit on the camp. It excused me from some other unpleasant duty, fire drill I think it was. I was also detailed to appear on the stage of one of the large cinemas in Derby in a patriotic display of the war effort. All the services were involved. In an unpatriotic moment I caught German measles and spent two weeks or more in an isolation ward in a Derby hospital. This did give me a few days sick leave at home which was some recompense.

My 21st birthday was in June 1940 and unfortunately

there was no hope of getting home. Mother and Father sent me some money and I managed to get into Derby and bought a new wristwatch to mark the occasion. By this time I had got to know a local young lady rather well and later that summer I managed to get some leave and took Marjorie home. I was able to hire a car from Keeling's Garage, opposite our home in Greenstead Road, which we enjoyed for a couple of days even though petrol had risen to 1s 6d a gallon. I think the end of that leave was the last time I saw Father.

In late September 1940, Knights, my fellow carpenter got sent home on embarkation leave prior to being posted overseas. Naturally I was rather pleased it was him and not me. On the day he should have returned, the admin office received a telegram confirming he was too ill to travel. Within hours I was being inoculated and cleared for the overseas posting in his place. The inspection was thorough and not like the oft-quoted brief encounter with the medical officer who, with hand on the victim's forearm, was said to pronounce: "You are warm. A1 for overseas."

I went by rail to St. Pancras station, London, and the platform was covered in broken glass from the previous evening's bombing. Then it was on to Uxbridge for two or three days' final kitting-out with tropical clothing, and meeting other members of the group. I also found time to write home to tell my family I had no idea where I was going, what was happening and that the next time they heard from me I would be somewhere overseas. Rumours abounded but noone knew our destination.

I have often thought what a shock the whole business must have been for Mother and Father but there was nothing I could do to ease things or even give them more information, not that we had much ourselves. There was no appeal against the posting. The medical officer had pronounced me fit for overseas posting and that was final. In a way I was luckier than some of the group. Several had only recently married and they must have been feeling pretty miserable.

To Liverpool and the ship that was to transport us somewhere overseas. She was SS Pasteur, a luxury liner that had been nearing completion in a French shipyard when war broke out. As the Nazis cut through Holland and Belgium, it was decided to move her to prevent her from being seized. Her maiden voyage was three months early: she left Brest on June 2, 1940, for Halifax, Nova Scotia, carrying 300 tons of gold bullion from French banks.

In Canada, the Pasteur was converted into a troopship and sailed for England with a number of Commonwealth soldiers. Although her conversion had altered much of her interior it was still possible to appreciate what a beautiful ship she was, in spite of the awful smell from the French cigarettes that the Canadians must have been smoking. At Liverpool, she took on a contingent of British soldiers and our smaller group of RAF personnel. We were berthed at the ocean liner terminal near the Liver Building and I remember standing on deck late in the afternoon of our arrival from Uxbridge, looking across the Mersey, speculating on the future and gathering my thoughts of the last few days that had seen such a dramatic turnaround in my life.

We left the next day, October 30, 1940, at about 9am, a grey miserable wet day bound for the Clyde to pick up more soldiers. On October 31 we left Glasgow, our destination unknown. Because the Pasteur was a fast ship, no escorts were provided and alone we headed out into the north Atlantic. That area is no mill-pond and I was very seasick but still had to parade on deck each day for safety drill. We in the RAF had comfortable bunks but the Army was much worse off. The Army contingent was quite large and their accommodation in the lower decks was much more utilitarian than ours. Their toilets were no more than a trough with a row of seats arranged across the deck. This trough was built with a slope and there was a steady flow of water to flush away sewage. It did not take long for some wag to create havoc by launching a burning paper boat at the high end, waiting for the howls as the little fireship passed beneath his colleagues' tender parts. Service life was never dull. The fun and anger, and other emotions, held us together.

As we edged our way southwards the weather improved greatly and, feeling much better, I was able to appreciate the sunshine and the deep blue of the sea. We were kept amused by the tales told by two of our number, one who had been a stage electrician at the Windmill Theatre, London, and the other who had fitted furniture in homes of the better-off. I suppose in a way we had been educated. At least our minds were broadened by some of the tales they told. We arrived at Gibraltar six days after leaving the Clyde but were not allowed on deck until it was dark. This was to stop German spies watching from the Spanish shore noting down troop movements.

Our RAF contingent was split into small groups and put aboard the ships of a convoy escort. I was allocated to the destroyer HMS Faulkner, the flotilla leader, and put in the communications mess. This was towards the bow and low down, and once we were under way we saw no daylight through the portholes because of the speed we moved through the water.

I noted in my diary: "Although I was seasick I had quite

The liner Pasteur. She did sterling service as a troopship in the Second World War and later for the French in Indochina. In 1957 she was bought by a German line and renamed Bremen. She sank in the Indian Ocean in 1980 on her way to the breaker's yard.

Courtesy of simplonpc.co.uk

A Fairey Swordfish used by the Fleet Air Arm in Malta. These torpedo bombers, known as stringbags, were out of date by 1939 but achieved spectacular successes including crippling the battleship Bismarck.

Thinking of you — Mother had this family picture taken especially to send to me in Malta. Father and Mother are left and right, Joan and Ken at the back, and Jean at the front.

Meet the boys! I am pictured at the front on the right with other members of my unit in Malta.

Ready for splashdown. A Short Sunderland flying boat on the slipway at Kalafrana. These planes were used as patrol bombers against U-boats.

The opera house in Valletta, opened in 1866, lies in ruins after an air raid in 1942. The site has still to be redeveloped.

Clearing up after air raids became a way of life. The aim was to rescue survivors then remove the rubble to the sides of the streets to allow traffic to pass again.

This Short Sunderland seaplane was caught at her moorings in Kalafrana by a Messerschmitt Bf 109...

...smoke billows across the bay as the fire engulfs the aircraft...

...as the plane settles into the harbour, the
water puts out the fire...

...finally, only the aircraft tail is visible.
The event was over in minutes.

a good time because of the kindheartedness of the sailors." These wonderful men collected food from the galley and brought it down to us, and did their best to ease our passage. They were concerned at my violent seasickness and did their best to get some food inside me, so that I wasn't retching on an empty stomach. One sailor suggested I swallow a lump of fat meat tied to a piece of string so I could be sick without harm to my innards. Those navy lads were great characters.

As we moved through the narrow passage between the island of Pantelleria and Sicily we were subjected to air and sea attacks from the Italians but luckily there were no major casualties. Thank goodness the Germans had not at that time arrived in Sicily. Any anxiety that I might have felt about the attacks was submerged beneath my continuing and awful seasickness.

Where were we going? For the whole journey we had no idea and only found out when the sailors on the deck of the destroyer pointed out the small island of Malta on the horizon.

We disembarked in Grand Harbour late afternoon on November 10, and a bigger contrast to the wet and miserable Liverpool we had left behind would have been hard to find. Warm sunshine, cream-coloured stone buildings, friendly people and no sense of the awfulness of war that was apparent in London and Liverpool. It was soon to change!

After a hair-raising ride in one of the local buses we finally arrived at Hal-far, a Fleet-Air Arm airfield (now it is part of the runway of the Luqa air terminal). No-one seemed sure what to do with us and we had five days of kicking our heels. We easily got passes to leave camp and visited Valletta, the island capital. It was still almost like peace-time and we had

Air raid on HMS Illustrious in Valetta. She survived and eventually reached Alexandria.

a pleasant time with afternoon tea in Blackley's restaurant, which was so typically English. On November 16 I and several others were posted to Kalafrana, a sea-plane and air-sea rescue launch base. I found Kalafrana to be much the same as the base at Felixstowe where I had my weekend training. The same hangars, slipways, electric crane and barrack blocks. I almost felt at home.

The barracks were pretty spartan, the beds definitely so! I think they were called McDonald beds. The springing was flat steel strips and the mattresses were two or three hard pads about three inches thick laid on the steel strips. The bottom half of the bed was pushed under the top half during the day to make more room. Each barrack room had a paraffin-fired brazing torch and it became part of a weekly routine to play the torch over the steel frame and springs to kill the bed-bugs, fleas and cockroaches. We used to stand the legs of the bed in boot polish tins filled with paraffin to stop bugs crawling up.

The period from my arrival in Malta in November 1940 to early January 1941 was the lull before the storm. We did have the occasional high-level bombing raid from the Italians but they were of little account. Work was easy, mainly the repair and maintenance of air-sea rescue boats and launches, and we had a fair amount of time off, often spent in Valletta. In the workshops we had a large number of Maltese tradesmen. These men could be temperamental: one morning we were missing a carpenter and later found that he was in jail, having killed a man in a bar the evening before. Their skills never ceased to amaze me, however. They would work on a long piece of timber using an adze, producing a surface as smooth as if it had been machine-planed. I was occasionally taken out for an evening's fishing by one of these men. We would row to one of the areas he knew well and would throw overboard 4-inch squares of cork, to each of which was attached a baited hook. All we had to do was to enjoy the calm of the evening and watch for an animated square, knowing then that a fish had taken the bait. Those carefree occasions did not last long but the happy memories are still with me.

On December 5 I received my kit-bag which had been transported separately from me, and that enabled me to have a much-needed change of clothes. The corporal in charge of the section was a peace-time member of the air force and, with his wife, had been in Malta for a long time. Corporal Blowers and Dot lived off the station in a flat and until they were posted home they were kind to me in many ways, offering the comforts of home life when I had time off. A note in my diary for November 1941 reads: "Hot bath at Charlie and Dot's, the first for ten months." This dear couple provided many a good meal not only to me but others from the unit.

On November 24 I was detailed to be a member of a funeral escort and this caused me considerable disquiet. I had never experienced the usual square-bashing that new recruits had so I was ignorant of service drill except for "attention", "at ease" and left or right turn. Of rifle drill I knew nothing. Help was soon at hand, however, and two long-service corporals soon had me well prepared, practising with a broom. The next day I reported for duty and Lady Luck smiled: I found I was a pallbearer and so did not have to bear arms.

Late 1940 marked a change in the war in Malta as the Germans moved into Sicily. By January 1941 bombing was almost non-stop and between New Year 1942 and July 24,

1942, there was only one period of 24 hours without bombs.

The workshops at Kalafrana were fully occupied with repairs helping to keep the aircraft serviceable at Luqa, Hal-far and Ta-Qali. In September 1941 it was decided to disperse some of the facilities. A unit was moved to Gzira where we took over Muscat's garage and showroom, and a bus depot farther along the road. We were billeted in a block of flats fronting the bus depot.

I became responsible for the repair of air-screw blades and had a unit in Muscat's garage. Together with a clever Maltese civilian named Baldachino we developed a way of joining salvaged blade parts that was superior to the official method and our idea was eventually accepted. It was usually a case of one good blade from two damaged blades. I also had to go out at times to do repairs to planes at dispersal sites.

I note from my diary:

1941

February 6, 7 - Hurricane repairs at Dingli.

February 10 - six air-raids

February 13 - seven air-raids

Life was often uncomfortable, at times pretty hair-raising and sometimes damned frightening. We were marginally away from the main targets although the submarine depot on Manoel Island was only down the road. Life had its compensations. We were away from the more disciplined and formal regime at Kalafrana and as a small unit we enjoyed a friendly and informal existence.

After several months at the more heavily-bombed part of the island we were given seven days leave at a rest villa at St Paul's Bay. My turn came in July 1941 and along with about a dozen others we relaxed with some swimming, sleeping

Close-up to a Hurricane — the plane was in for impromptu repairs at Dingli air-strip.

and enjoying the company of two Maltese sisters Ann and Doris Ellul. Unfortunately after two or three days I went down with dysentery and was packed off to Imtarfa Hospital where I remained for 12 days.

Food was often on our mind. The menu would vary as and when a convoy got through. I remember some Australian margarine and canned sausages which were pretty good. Maconochie was a staple — this was a canned meat and vegetable stew — and of course we had bully beef. We had hard tack biscuits and some Navy-issue chocolate bar which was hard and not too sweet. By breaking up a couple of biscuits in a mug and leaving the pieces to soak, then scraping some of the chocolate and biscuit mix together, and applying some heat, we had a passable chocolate pudding. Even cold it was fairly palatable. I only remember two items I found it almost impossible to swallow. One was dehydrated banana which was black when mixed with water and the other was some rice that, rumour had it, was salvaged from a watery grave. We had a free issue of 50 cigarettes fairly regularly, some of them obscure brands from Egypt. As a non-smoker I was easily able to swap the cigarettes for a bread ration, which at that time was about half a small loaf a week.

In spite of work and the air-raids we did manage to visit the cinema occasionally. Although the films were mostly ones we had seen at home it was still a change from work, in spite of the interruptions caused by the raids.

The air-raids were more or less continuous but not always at our end of the island. January 5, 1942, was notable as our first peaceful night for five weeks.

One particular raid occasioned a lot of distress both in the unit and personally. We had the garage and the bus depot for workshops, and the flats we lived in were in front of the bus depot. One evening a great friend, Syd Parmenter, along with one or two others decided to sleep in the basement of the garage along the road because they thought it would be safer. I declined an invitation to join them. Sadly the garage got a direct hit and Syd was killed. It was a sobering time because we had all slept at the garage when we were on guard or fire-picket duties.

Malta was receiving so much attention from the Germans because it could be seen as their stepping stone from Europe to Africa and the Middle East. After the collapse of France it was the Allies' only base in the Mediterranean between Gibraltar and Alexandria in Egypt. This tiny island was a barrier to Hitler's ambition to take north Africa and the Middle East oilfields, and sweep east to link up with the Japanese. That Churchill was so committed to holding on to Malta was proof of its importance. And so life continued through 1941 and 1942. We did receive mail but irregularly and quite often it was late or very late. When it came it was often a mixed blessing — the elation of news of home and loved ones, and then the reaction as we thought of the miles between us. However, we were young and we had a unique bond of friendship to sustain us. Those who have not served in war under difficult and dangerous conditions, where your friend of the morning may be dead by the evening, cannot understand the feeling that held us together. The shared sympathies, shared laughter and the knowledge that you were not alone and that you depended on each other. That, and those we left behind, is what we remember on Armistice Day.

Our deepest sympathies were for those poor fellows who received a Dear John note. This was a letter from a loved one, wife or sweetheart, to break the news that he was no longer the man in her life and he was not the father of the new baby. These letters were devastating and I am sure the senders never fully understood the cruelty of what they were doing. Some men literally went to pieces, especially if they happened to hear the Vera Lynn song, Yours.

In late December 1942 I was summoned to the admin office and told that I was going home on a compassionate posting. Father was seriously ill and had been asking to see me, and somehow Mother had managed to find a way to get me home. I often wonder if Mother's Maltese doctor had some influence. It was a rush job to say farewells, get the necessary clearance papers and be ready for the flight from Luqa. In the event the flight was full and I had to wait for the next one two days later.

We left Malta during the night in a twin-engined Beaufort as darkness gave a better chance of avoiding enemy aircraft. We arrived at Gibraltar the next morning. No seats, no parachute, we sat on the floor on our kit-bags. I can still remember looking out as we flew over the northern part of north Africa and seeing small points of light which we were told were locals' camp fires. Gibraltar was an eye-opener after Malta. It was unscathed by bombing, its shops were open with goods to sell, the bars were doing a roaring trade and steaks were available in the cafes. My enjoyment of the moment was overshadowed by the desire to get home to see Father. Unfortunately no flight to the UK was available and I had to embark on a cargo ship. I chose to sleep on deck because I thought it might be safer in the event of a torpedo attack. I arrived in the UK in early January 1943 and as soon as I could I let Mother know by telegram, but I was too late. Father had died a week or two before. I felt sorrow for myself but more so for Father who had so much wanted to see me before he died. War is cruel in many ways.

I mentioned earlier that while in Derby I had met and cultivated the acquaintance of a local girl. Marjorie and I corresponded as far as conditions would allow while I was in Malta and all seemed to be going well and I was looking forward to a happy reunion. As there was no pressure to reach home now that Father had been buried I arranged with Mother that I would call in to Derby to see Marjorie and then continue to Colchester.

When Marjorie came to the door to greet me I realised that if I had still been in Malta I would have been receiving a Dear John. There was no doubt that Marjorie was pregnant. Mother, God Bless her, must have been informed of the situation and had travelled up to Derby to be there and to help me over the shock. I think a Canadian serviceman was involved. Altogether not the best of homecomings.

A few days leave and I was posted to Stradishall in Suffolk, to a maintenance unit modifying and preparing gliders for D-Day. This was a complete change to Malta. No airraids, adequate food and the chance to get home on days off. Trains were still running then on the Colne Valley line and I could catch the train at Haverhill, travelling through Halstead to Colchester. Stradishall had its down side, however. Stricter discipline meant "short, back and sides" haircuts and RAF police insisting your hat was worn properly. This was a regulation that I fell foul of, and I was put on a charge. Luckily, the NCO in the guard-room was my barber in Civvy Street: only a reprimand followed.

During 1942 I had started to get a wheezy chest at times, for no apparent reason. At Gzira we were under the Army for messing and medical care and the Army MO prescribed menthol inhalations which gave slight relief. The symptoms would come and go and I was inclined to put it down to the conditions we were living under. However the attacks of breathlessness persisted at Stradishall and the station MO referred me to the RAF hospital at Littleport in Cambridgeshire. Transport was provided by the station for me and several others. The driver was a WAAF, a member of the Women's Auxiliary Air Force, and I incurred that young lady's displeasure when the car stopped for no apparent reason, and I asked if she had checked the petrol before leaving! I was forgiven and an invitation to the station cinema was accepted. From then on Elsie Lunn and I spent as much time together as we could and eventually realised how much we meant to each other. Once our relationship was going well, I could not resist calling Elsie "Sally", after the original Sally Lunn who a made a type of yeast-bread bun, known as a Sally Lunn bun, in Bath in the 17th century. I don't think the allusion to a bun was appreciated at first, even though Sally did not like her first name. Before long, however, "Sally" began to be used between us, and Sally she remained until her death in 2002.

We married in September 1943 and for a while lived in lodgings with a family in Haverhill. After a short time at Stradishall the unit was posted to Wratting Common, a satellite aerodrome, and then to Tarrant Rushton, Dorset. This base was involved in the build-up for D-Day. We had two classes of gliders, the big Hamilcars and the smaller troop-carrying Horsas. The tugs were Halifaxes. We also had some involvement with preparations for Special Operations Executive missions. There was great secrecy and we knew nothing of what was happening apart from flights at unusual times and strange coming and goings, As D-Day approached all leave was cancelled and everyone confined to camp. This continued for some time after D-Day.

My daughter Brenda was born on June 27 and shortly afterwards restrictions were relaxed and I was able to get a 24-hour pass to visit Sally and baby. During the later stages of her pregnancy Sally had been living with her parents in London. Her maternity unit had been evacuated from London to Tyringham House, near Newport Pagnell, Buckinghamshire, which was quite a journey from Dorset, particularly in view of the restrictions on public transport. I reached London by hitching lifts, caught a train to Wolverton and then by lift and a long walk reached Tyringham House after being caught in a thunderstorm. As it was already late in the day I was unable to stay for long. It was sufficient time, however, to hold the baby, and hug my wife. For any man, holding his first-born is a unique experience. It is an incredible feeling to see that cherubic face, downy hair and

Sally and me — my joke about checking on the petrol in her car led to a date at the cinema …and marriage

perfect hands and feet. It is truly a touch of heaven. While the memory of that moment has lasted a lifetime, my visit was brief. Sally and I probably discussed the baby's name but that was it; there was little hope of seeing them again for some time to come.

Getting back to camp by 8am the next day was a problem. I got to Wolverton station all right and had food and drink at the Salvation Army canteen (what a blessing the SA was) and managed to catch a train to London. I knew there was a fast train from Waterloo just before midnight that would get me to Salisbury and with luck I caught it. Blandford Forum was a large Army centre 20 miles from Salisbury and I thought the chances of a lift were good. Once in Blandford I knew I could pick up a lift into camp which was only a few miles away. My good luck ran out at Salisbury, no lifts and I was forced to the conclusion that I would have to walk it — which I did. It was an eerie walk, passing through villages with not a chink of light anywhere, just the odd vehicle going the other way. Not another soul did I meet or pass, though I got soaked in another storm. I reached camp on time but I was dead beat. The sergeant with whom I worked was a kindly soul and after I reported for work he implied that I should get lost until mid-day. Sleeping quarters could not be used due to CO's inspection and so I climbed into the cock-pit of a Hamilcar glider in the hangar, settled down and had three or four hours sleep knowing my work crew would keep unwanted visitors at bay.

As the war in Europe reached its end our workload gradually eased and restrictions were lifted. Sally and Brenda joined me after I found accommodation in Wimborne, and for a while we also had Sally's younger brother Roy with us. Wimborne was a much quieter place than London. We were able to get the train to Bournemouth when I had a day off and in Bobbie's restaurant it was still possible to get afternoon tea, but without fancy cakes.

VE day found me in the RAF hospital at Yatesbury for I was still having problems with my breathing. Sally and Brenda were back in London with Sally's parents and after discharge from Yatesbury all thoughts were on demobilisation.

When my name came up, I had to report to the demob depot, which I think was Uxbridge, Middlesex, to get kitted out for civvy street. A new suit, shoes, hat, shirt and various items of my RAF clothing, a discharge book and my bounty which was just over £90.

So ended my RAF career. Six years of normal life lost but the balance sheet was not all on the debit side. I had shared in some unique and, at times, life-threatening activities. I had met and enjoyed the friendship of men and women from a wide and varied cross-section of society. My eyes had been opened and my mind enriched. I was certainly wiser and more knowledgeable of my fellow creatures and the world that existed beyond the rural confines of pre-war Greenstead, and the market town of Colchester.

I realised that none of us could go back to the way of life that we had been forced to leave in 1939. Some of the threads could be picked up but many had been broken for ever.

One thing was certain. After six years of having every moment constrained and directed by service rules and discipline we were now free, but we had a future to create. I looked forward to the challenge.

Back to Brackett's

I returned to Brackett's in March 1946. Much had changed but much had not. My wage had gone up to £7 10s, and the union had struck a deal to end Saturday working, though this meant longer working days during the week. Overall, though, our week went down from 48 hours to less than 43. The personnel were mostly the same people I had left in 1939, and there was now a works canteen and the workshop had more machinery. If I was to continue in engineering I had to get some qualifications in engineering patternmaking and foundry work, so I began evening classes at the Technical College, aiming for City and Guilds and the Institute of Mechanical Engineer exams.

Sally, Brenda and I initially lived with Mother but it was crowded and we moved in with Aunt Hilda and Grandmother. Sally was persistent in worrying the Colchester Council housing department and in late 1946 we were offered a flat in a converted house in Military Road, Colchester.

We had the top floor of three. Because of shortages in the aftermath of war, fitting out the flat was difficult. We had tokens to buy so-called utility furniture whenever the shops had supplies. Utility furniture was plain but well made; it was created under government control to make the best use of restricted supplies. We had ours for several years.

Sally spent many hours going round the town while I was at work keeping an eye out for items that might appear in the shops, including off-ration food. In many ways it was fun and I think we had much more satisfaction getting a home together during those often difficult times than do today's young couples with everything to hand. We really did have orange boxes with curtains covering them to provide storage.

The winter of early 1947 was cold, the only heating was from small open fires in lofty and draughty rooms, but we were lucky: we had our own place. When the water supply froze we had to make do with a milk churn of water that Mr Watts the dairy-man next door kindly provided. The toilet and bathroom were both off the landing of the flat and the bathroom, especially, would have made a good frozen food store.

Hot water came from a large copper geyser suspended over one end of the bath. The gas lit when the tap at its base turned the water on, and the noise of ignition reverberated through the flat. The toilet was separate and had a solid wooden door with a sliding bolt for privacy and no window.

Brenda, at three years old, found one day that she could reach the bolt, could even slide it along, but to her dismay could not slide it back! Result: a slightly damaged door after our efforts to rescue her.

Our neighbour over the road was the Army, on the other side of a 6ft wall. We had the bugle call of Reveille to wake us and the Last Post to see us to bed. From our front windows we could look over the parade ground and I often thought back 20 years or so to when father would walk us up on Sundays to see a colourful church parade.

When Sally became pregnant again we realised the flat was not going to be suitable and we asked to be moved to a two-bedroom property. Sally was marvellous. While I was at work she walked miles pushing Brenda in the pram round the various council offices arguing our case. Due in no small measure to her persistence, we were given a new prefab in King George Road in late 1947. It was heaven after the flat. Two bedrooms, bathroom and toilet, dining room-lounge and kitchen, all complete with hot water and cooker and fridge in the kitchen. There was a good-sized garden and a small shed for my bicycle and the pram, near the back door.

Marion, a cuddly and contented baby, was born in March 1948 in the old maternity home in Lexden Road. I was not there: it was not allowed in those days. I remember the weather was warm and sunny and I was busy laying a lawn in the back garden, and I cycled to the maternity home each afternoon to see Sally and Marion.

Work and study meant life was busy. I finished at Brackett's at 5.40pm Monday to Friday and it was a rush to cycle home, have tea, clean up and be at the Tech for 6.30pm, which I did for four nights of the week at one time. Gordon Ambridge, a friend from pre-war scouting, was studying for some of the same exams and on Friday evenings we alternated visiting each other to compare notes, study past question papers and explore answers. For many of my exams I had to take time off from work and my wages were deducted accordingly.

I had been well received by everyone at Brackett's but after six years of war I found it hard to settle. As a married man with a family, serious consideration had to be given to the future. By 1947 I had decided to become a teacher of handicraft, as it was then known. Further courses at college followed but this time with a career in education in mind.

1947-1948 was a turning point in our lives. I had done well in my exams, and top grades in my teachers' papers meant I could apply for an uncertificated teachers post. If I held this successfully for six months I could then apply for registration as a fully certificated teacher.

I left Brackett's and the engineering industry in December 1948 and the next month began my teaching career at East Ward School, Colchester. My annual salary was £386. In retrospect I have absolutely no regrets.

Learning to be a Teacher

At East Ward School I was under the tutelage of Larry Howarth. A better person to introduce me to the classroom and to teaching I could not have met. He showed me how to achieve discipline in a quiet but authoritative manner, the value of lesson preparation and the importance of personal presentation. I owe Larry a great debt of gratitude,

My probation went well and in May I received notification from the Ministry that from November 1 1949 I would be recognised as a fully qualified teacher. A milestone indeed, and both Sally and I were overjoyed that the years of studying had proved worthwhile.

My terms of employment linked me to the education authority, not one school. In June, I was moved from East Ward to a split post covering two schools, one in West Mersea and the other in Great Bentley — two days at one, three at the other. They were both all-standard schools with pupils from infants to seniors, and some distance from Colchester.

The school at West Mersea was in a mixture of old and new buildings. It had a strong rural science bias with extensive cultivated gardens, a small piggery and poultry sheds. I taught art and craft and woodwork, mainly to the boys, and enjoyed my time there. The staff were friendly and the headmaster supportive. My classroom was heated by an open fire and in that winter, 1949/50, for some reason we ran short of fuel. On the headmaster's suggestion I took some of the senior boys to the gardens and we went round cutting out dead wood from the trees which we split into logs for fuel. Not very educational in today's high-tech terms but the boys gained a sense of achievement and enjoyed a warm classroom.

Teachers' dinner duty entailed supervising the dining-hall, seeing that plates were cleared and each table clean for the second sitting. Meals were 6d and good value. The staff had their dinner in the staff room but vinegar was not allowed: the headmaster was a devout Methodist and banned it because of its association with the brewing industry. At Great Bentley conditions were somewhat similar, again with a strong rural science side. The fox hunt would meet on the village green and we used to take the school out to enjoy seeing the riders and hounds. It was a picturesque occasion.

The Bentley headmaster was a great believer in astrology and one afternoon he happened to accompany me on the train on the way home to Colchester. He asked me several questions about my attitude to things and then informed me that I was a Gemini and my birthday was between late May and late June — quite right! Thinking about it afterwards I could not see how he knew my birthday prior to our meeting on the train as I had not given any personal details to the school. A mystery, but it did not cause me to believe in astrology.

I did not have a car so I caught the bus to West Mersea, with the bus stop only a short distance from home. The morning bus was never held up by flooding on the Strood — the causeway out to the island — but it was delayed on some afternoons. To get to Great Bentley I caught the train from Colchester Hythe station, so this meant a cycle ride of a couple of miles, leaving my bicycle at Mother's home. It was an interesting and enjoyable time, apart from a few wintry mornings.

At this point I decided to do a year at college to augment my teaching qualification, so in July 1950 I left West Mersea and Great Bentley. I was accepted by one of the colleges set up after the war under the technical teacher training scheme, which required a degree-level entry. This was in London and it meant considerable disruption to family life: apart from holidays, I only saw Sally, Brenda and Marion at weekends. I used to travel by a Grey-Green company coach, and the return fare was 7/6. To catch it each Monday I had to leave King George Road before 6am to get to the High

Street for 6.30am. On the return journey on Friday evenings I could get a corporation bus from High Street if I was not too late. Students at the college were all mature, having been in the services or worked in the defence industry. They were a great group and amid all the work we had much fun. On one occasion we found that the psychology lecturer was monitoring the books lent by the library, presumably for his own research. We each agreed to take out a book featuring sex, the more erotic, the better. We heard later that he took it in good part.

During the Christmas holiday I managed to get relief work with the Post Office. This was to be repeated at other Christmases to supplement funds. In the summer I did holiday work as bread delivery van driver with Mr Ennew at Alresford. The area covered by the bread round included the villages all round Alresford and I usually managed to have a break on the quay at Wivenhoe. It was a challenge to drive the van on occasions — the gearbox was faulty and would not stay in second gear so I had to drive with one hand on the wheel and the other holding the lever in gear.

During this period I also built a television set. It was from a kit of parts supplied by Premier Radio of London made up from Government surplus stores which came on the market after the war. It had a six-inch screen and the picture had a greenish tinge. We were one-up on the neighbours even though the picture was small. The aerial was a large letter 'H' on top of a 30ft scaffold pole in the garden. On cup-final day we had several neighbours in to watch the game.

Moving Schools

After the year at college I decided to try for a post away from Essex, and I started at an all-boys' school in Ambleside Avenue, Walton-on-Thames, Surrey, in September 1951.

The housing situation was difficult to say the least. Council housing was only available for long-time residents, especially those returning from military service. London County Council was developing some estates several miles away but the chances of even getting on the waiting list were remote, and it became obvious we would have to buy. Even that option was limited as the supply of new homes was tightly controlled by a system of building permits, and this meant that older properties did not often come on to the market.

It was 12 months before the family were able to join me. During that year I lived for a while with Sally's parents, John and Elsie, at Glengarnock Avenue, Millwall, London, travelling by train to Walton from Waterloo, while Sally and the girls stayed at the pre-fab in Colchester. My daily journey involved walking through the Greenwich foot tunnel and then catching a tram. During this time, the trams were replaced by buses and I kept the special ticket printed to mark the passing of trams in London.

The school was a happy one with strong traditions of service and civility coupled with high educational attainment. It had all-male staff except for one woman, the only female left from the large number who had filled staff vacancies during the war. The headmaster, Mr Wilcox, was a gentleman in all senses of the term and I came to consider my time there as some of the happiest and most rewarding of my teaching career.

There were two handicraft rooms, I had one and the other was held by John Hammond, whose parents lived in Wivenhoe. The school had a strong drama tradition and John and I were involved with the art and science department in providing scenery, lighting and props for shows. At one time we needed some electrical equipment that we thought might be available from the shops in London that were disposing of government war surplus. I volunteered to obtain it on one of my trips home and was given an address in Soho. I later found it was a street that was in the news as the centre of a prostitution racket, and my volunteering led to a lot of ribaldry. However, I had wandered the whole street looking for the electrical gear and was not propositioned once.

Being based in London I was finding it difficult to house-hunt in Walton, so I moved to New Haw, near Weybridge, to share a flat with John, and I started to look for houses in earnest.

House prices in Walton-on-Thames were higher than in Colchester by about 20% but we did eventually find one in the Hersham area. Buying the house was quite a problem because the building societies at that time were strict over how much they would advance. I think 75% was their maximum, which meant that on the price of £1,950 I had to find nearly £500, a fair bit of money. The solicitor I had was supportive and with his help I managed to obtain loans from the British Legion and the Royal Air Force Association that enabled me to get the deposit together and we moved in during August 1952.

We enjoyed living at Hersham. The house was within cycling distance of school — for me! Brenda had to catch a bus to get to her junior school and I used to take Marion on the crossbar of my bike to the infants' school which was near my own. The town was well served by public transport and we could easily shop in Kingston-upon-Thames or be in the West End of London in just over half-an-hour.

With Brenda and Marion both at school, Sally took a part-time job in the school meals service which fitted in with school holidays. It was here that Sally met May Elliott who, with Dennis her husband, became great friends. Dennis worked for a company that provided him with a van, and we had many outings with four adults and three children crammed into it.

My salary had gone up and I remember my take-home cheque in 1952/53 was £45, which we divided into three. £15 to mortgage, £15 to Sally for housekeeping and £15 for other expenses. I also worked on Saturdays in a shop in Walton helping to repair radios and televisions, and taught at evening classes. While working in the shop I managed to get a cheap secondhand 9-ins black and white television on which we watched the coronation of Queen Elizabeth. It was a big improvement on our original six-inch set, especially when I bought a plastic magnifier lens to place in front of the screen.

I enjoyed my job at Walton-on-Thames but knew I would have to move to further my career. We also had to fit this in with Brenda and Marion's education and tried to time any change to coincide with them stepping up from infants to junior, or junior to secondary. Brenda was a hard worker and we were delighted when she was selected for grammar school. This was obviously the time for a move and in May 1955 I started a new job at Stevenage in Hertfordshire.

New Town Experience

Stevenage, an old market town on the A1 which used to be known as the Great North Road, had been designated a New Town under the terms of the 1946 Act. It was expanding hugely and new schools were being built for the increasing number of children. My job was as head of handicrafts in a brand new school and I had the summer term to organise the department — ordering all the equipment for both woodwork and metalwork — before the first intake in September.

Housing was not a problem: it was provided by the Housing Corporation and we had the choice of several houses, all new. We decided on one in Broadwater Crescent. It was one of the more expensive homes, it gave us more room and it had the advantage that Brenda's and Marion's schools were nearby. All houses were rented and I think we were paying about £16 a month for the house. Selling-up in Surrey gave us a little capital and we decided to buy a car, a secondhand Hillman Minx which cost us £225.

The pupils were an interesting mixture. Stevenage was absorbing a large number of families from the eastern side of London, and the secondary schools also had to take in pupils from the rural communities around the town, so classes were an interesting cross-section ranging from rural boys and girls to city-slicker, know-it-all types. The headmaster became aware of something "going on" on the buses used to bring the country children to school. As a strict Methodist, the truth came as a shock: the boys, egged on by the girls, were using a ruler to boast of their manhood. We never did find out which boy got top honours.

With everything being new it was important for the school to foster a spirit of community and the parent/teacher association was a good one. Many of the pupils' fathers were in the construction industry and helped with one of the major projects: the building of a swimming pool complete with treatment plant. This required a great deal of my time, particularly at weekends.

Another member of staff, a Mr Guest, and myself formed a cinema club and we put on a show one evening a week in the school hall. We had two 16mm film projectors and built a small projection booth. We showed full length films with synchronised change-overs from reel to reel. Our evening programme would be one full-length film, one short and at least one cartoon. The school tuck shop sold sweets and ice-cream in the interval and our audiences would usually number well over 100.

Hertfordshire Educational Foundation had a facility at Stalham in Norfolk for schools to take groups sailing on Barton Broad. With the headmaster's agreement I used to apply for a week's booking and was usually allocated a week near Easter. We had the mixture of warm sunshine, thunderstorms, cold winds and frost but the sailing was good in spite of that.

Living in Stevenage had many good things about it but it was a long way from saltwater and sailing. Brenda was readying herself for O-levels in a year or so while Marion appeared to have a good chance of passing the eleven-plus exam. It was time to think of moving on, perhaps for the final move in my career. We decided to try to return to Colchester as it would be easier to see Mother and certainly no more difficult to visit Sally's parents, so in 1958 I applied for a post with North East Essex Education Authority.

Back in Essex

New secondary schools were in the pipeline to cope with the so-called baby boomers, and Essex was no exception. I was lucky enough to be appointed to a school which had no buildings: they were to be ready in 1960. In the meantime Monkwick School was accommodated in the Grey Friars building on East Hill in Colchester, recently vacated by the Girls' High School. Our two years in Grey Friars were very enjoyable. It was a lovely old building with gardens at the back. The girls had to wear indoor shoes rather than heels as the hardwood floors were the pride and joy of the caretaker, a Mr Bailey. He must have been heartbroken when the school that followed us into the premises declared the floors a safety hazard. After all his years of care, the floors were sanded and roughened.

Sally and I had to start house hunting again and it was obvious we would have to buy. We secured a plot on a development by local builder W Hills at Prettygate, but the house would not be ready until early 1959. I had to start my job in September 1958 and it would be wise for Brenda to transfer to the Girls' High School at the same time, so from September 1958 to March 1959 Brenda and I spent weekends with Sally and Marion in Stevenage and during the week lived with Mother, my sister Jean and her husband Peter in Greenstead Road. By this time we had traded in the Minx for a newer Ford Anglia but we still had some rough winter journeys from Hertfordshire to Essex, leaving Stevenage at about 6am each Monday. On one foggy trip we came across a large cow in the middle of the road, probably more confused than we were.

Our new home cost £2,150 with the land, roughly equal to three times my salary. It was a three-bedroom detached house with garage at the Lexden end of The Commons. We were fortunate enough to know Mr Breen, a director of Hills the builders, as his daughter Susan had been a playmate of Brenda when we were last in Colchester. Mr Breen made sure we were satisfied with the house and agreed to several alterations, including central heating. To offset the increased cost I did the interior decorating myself.

My teaching now was fully taken up with technical and engineering drawing. While we were at the old buildings in Grey Friars I had a room looking across the garden to the Castle Park. I also did some form teaching and for this my room was at the front, opposite the bus park entrance. It was noisy in the summer if we wanted the windows open.

The school moved to its new buildings in 1960 on the edge of the Monkwick estate. Our catchment area extended to West Mersea and the places in between, and also included the living quarters of the staff of the Military Corrective Training Centre. Initially all went well but the actions of the education authority — all with the best of intentions — led to friction with Mersea parents when it became clear the island would not be given its own secondary school. The resentment felt by Mersea people often focused on us teachers and on the school itself, as if we were to blame for the fiasco. The resentment smouldered for a long time and some parents lost no opportunity to pour scorn on the school and try to run it down. It was all in vain as it was obvious the council was never going to build a secondary school on the island. As the name Monkwick was used in such a pejorative manner, it was decided to give the school a new identity. I was tasked with coming up with suggestions, and Thomas, Lord Audley; Archbishop Harsnett; Sir George Lisle, and Lord Fairfax were all considered. The majority vote was for Thomas, Lord Audley, and the name was adopted.

The school grew to about 500 pupils which I always felt was the best size, big enough to command adequate facilities yet small enough to give a family feeling; a close knit community. When the comprehensive system was introduced, the school roll increased to well over 1,000 and staff numbers doubled. Regrettably, the family atmosphere went, minor divisions occurred within the staff room, and the children became more distant.

Marriage Heartbreak

We settled back into Colchester in early 1959. I was enjoying school, Sally had a job in town and Brenda and Marion were both doing well at the Girls' High. I was getting a fair amount of sailing with Tom Davies, a teacher at Harwich, and with the school sailing group at West Mersea. I completed the building of an Enterprise dinghy that I had started in Stevenage. We had made good friends and all seemed well.

However, by late 1963, relations between Sally and myself had deteriorated, there was strain between us and I suspected Sally had become attached to one of the staff at Adams Motors in Culver Street, where she was working. On Saturday April 11, 1964, I returned from town to find Sally had left home to be with her colleague, Gerry Green.

That November Sally asked if we could try a reconciliation, but it was difficult; we tried but the damage had been done. In January 1965 Sally left and I began divorce proceedings after discussions with Brenda and Marion, and the decree was made final in October 1965 on the grounds of Sally's admitted adultery. It was a low period in my life; thank goodness I had Brenda and Marion for whose support I shall forever be grateful.

Meeting Megan

It was then that Megan came into my life. Megan, a widow, had joined our staff at school after completing her training as a mature student following the sudden death of her husband. On May 28, 1966, Megan and I were married at Colchester Register Office with a service of blessing at All Saints, Shrub End.

Megan had three children, Ann, David and Stanley. Integration did cause problems but nothing insurmountable and gradually things settled down. At this time, Brenda was married and no longer at home, while Marion was at college in London. Ann was at the Gilberd school, which was then on North Hill, Colchester, Stanley was at Home Farm primary school, Stanway, and David continued as a boarder at the Friends School, Saffron Walden. David, however, became increasingly unhappy and he eventually moved to the Gilberd school.

We had two houses between us, my home at The Commons, Colchester, and Megan's at Great Oakley, near Dovercourt. We decided to sell the older Oakley house as we both worked in Colchester and Marion, Ann and David were at school there. With some of the money from the Oakley house sale, we had a fourth bedroom and a sun lounge built on to the house in The Commons.

Sailing and Sunsets

Although I suffer from sea-sickness, I have always loved messing about in boats. Pre-war years in the Sea Scouts gave me some cherished times on the water. Now was the time for me to pass on my love of the sea.

The headmaster at Thomas, Lord Audley school was a keen sailor and encouraged fellow teacher Alan Coleman and myself to form a sailing club.

We started building a Torch dinghy in the school workshops which, when completed, we kept at West Mersea. Throughout the sailing season we had one evening each week when we joined other club members for training. Weekends were often spent participating in regattas organised by Essex Schools Sailing Association and the National Schools Sailing Association. We had some good sailors and carried off a goodly number of trophies.

We also took groups of boys on week-long seamanship

trips to TS Foudroyant in Portsmouth Harbour. There, they slept in hammocks, messed as the sailors used to, and had ex-Navy officers in charge. They practised sailing and rowing in and around the harbour and were taken to the Isle of Wight for a day in one of the ship's boats. Sometimes we were joined by boys from Sir Anthony Deane School, Harwich, or the Gilberd School, Colchester.

Megan was keen to sail and we joined Harwich and Dovercourt Sailing Club. Our first boat was Dawn Treader, a 27ft Eventide that we brought from Great Wakering to Brightlingsea then on to Harwich. Much of the trip via the Roach, the Crouch and the Ray Sand channel was under motor because of a lack of wind. Dawn Treader gave us enjoyment but her wooden hull meant a lot of maintenance, so we sold her and bought Sea-Mist of Mersea, a 24ft glass fibre Snapdragon. We then decided to try a motor-cruiser, and I bought a 26ft Colvic bare hull with just the engine and sterngear installed; over 18 months I fitted it out as a 2/4 berth cruiser. We called her Esperee and had some enjoyable hours ranging from Ipswich down to Maldon and many places in between. Golden hours were spent in Pin Mill, Tollesbury Creek, Osea Island, Heybridge Basin and Walton Backwaters. Perhaps the best times were those spent not far from home, enjoying sunset evenings moored in the Pyefleet Channel: a gin and tonic in hand, the occasional call of a wader on the tideline, and each other's company in harmony. Sheer heaven.

Canes and Comprehensives

In 1970 I was appointed deputy headmaster at Thomas,

Lord Audley and assumed responsibility for discipline and time-tabling, as well as day-to-day organisation. Caning was still the punishment for serious breaches of discipline and administering it to the boys was one of my responsibilities. Miss Ollis, the assistant deputy headmistress, took care of disciplining the girls. A caning was always given in my office, in the presence of another member of staff and all details entered in a punishment book that was examined at every school governors' meeting. In all the canings I had to give I cannot recall one case where a boy bore me any resentment. Perhaps it was because of the investigation conducted in the presence of the miscreant and the teacher concerned; if there was any doubt regarding the offence another type of punishment was imposed.

The headmaster Aubrey Green was in many ways ahead of his time. We had a school council in which elected pupils helped with ideas and criticism. Mock elections were held when local or national elections were taking place. Looked at from the 21st century there seems nothing unusual in these activities but 40 years ago they were far from the norm.

With the political decision to create comprehensives, the school roll went well above 1,000. There were gains with extra equipment and facilities but I felt much was lost. With an assembly hall capacity of about 500 it was impossible to have any form of common meeting; the school was split into manageable units which worked against the idea of "one school".

In 1977, I took over as headteacher. It was an interesting and enjoyable end to my career as I had decided to retire two years early. Megan was now teaching in Brightlingsea and with income-tax arrangements at the time we were paying almost as much in tax between us as Megan's annual salary, which was absurd. We talked it over and decided that Megan should carry on teaching as she needed to get in more service to secure a good pension, and I would take on some of the domestic chores. An interesting situation arose when I contacted the Labour Exchange to ask about continuing to pay my NI stamp. I told them I was retired but they insisted I was unemployed. Because I had retired early, they had no other category for me. Against my wishes, I had to "sign on", though I must admit that the unemployment pay was useful.

Looking back, I realise that my teaching career gave me tremendous satisfaction and the feeling of having done a worthwhile job. I think the 1940s to the mid 1970s were some of the most rewarding years in secondary education, perhaps because the scourges of political correctness and elitism were virtually unknown, and discipline and good behaviour were high priorities. Competitiveness was a normal part of school work. Good spelling was important and personal calculators were unknown.

Much has been made of the eleven-plus selective exam and its so-called divisive result, in which some pupils were labelled failures. The accusation of failure was a ploy by those who had ulterior political motives. The lefties would say: "You failed the 11-plus." We would ask: "Did you pass?" Pupils who did not pass the selection process could try again at 13 and we regularly had pupils who moved on at that age. For those who stayed with us the way was open to A-levels and we had successes. I remember some boys and girls who entered professional careers, and I still meet those who have their own businesses and who run successful businesses for other people. Regretfully a few showed promise in other directions and later provided copy for court reporters.

Enjoying Freedom

As Megan's and my children built their own lives, talk turned to moving to a smaller house or bungalow. There was a lucky escape with a new house we looked at in Peldon. We had almost signed the contract when Claude Polley, a friend and surveyor, discovered settlement cracks. In the end we settled on a town house at Fieldgate Dock in Brightlingsea, which had a view from the lounge down the creek towards East Mersea.

Our time at Fieldgate Dock was enjoyable but several aspects gave us cause for concern, particularly the lease and not having a garden. In 1984 we started to look around Brightlingsea for a new home. It was, however, a time of runaway property prices, and while we did well selling Fieldgate Dock we had problems with gazumping. I remember one bungalow we were keen on which we looked over in the morning and agreed a price with the owner. We came home to lunch, the owner informed the agent of the sale and the agent told her to raise the price by £5,000 which pushed it well beyond our limit. We eventually moved into Seaview Road.

The prospect of retirement envisages lots of spare hours — for some maybe that is the case. For me, time filled up to overflowing. Apart from helping to run the home and look after the garden with Megan, I tried to fit in painting, wood-turning, sailing and enjoying the company of family and friends. Nowadays there are books waiting to be read, lunches to have with friends and walks to be taken for the sheer enjoyment of being free. I even squeeze in time to read The Telegraph and try the crossword. Bored? Never ever.

I Love Holidays!

The big advantage of not working is being able to travel when you like. My lifetime has seen families' horizons expand from trips to Wales and the West Country to Europe and the rest of the world.

As life settled down after the second world war, like most people we spent our holidays in the UK. Our favoured venues were from Weymouth and Swanage down to Penzance and round to St Ives. No motorways then! We would leave home at about 4am to avoid heavy traffic and would drive straight through London, out on the A4 and then A3, A30 or A303 depending on our destination. Honiton and Exeter were notorious for jams and usually meant long delays.

When we lived at Fieldgate Dock much of our leisure time was spent caravanning and sailing with our neighbours Ralph and Irene Callan, and Joan Milman and daughters Lindsay and Mandy. Our big adventure was a 1974 trip to Las Palmas in the Canaries, our first "flying" holiday. We went from Gatwick airport with airline entrepreneur Freddie Laker. No subsequent flight, even those to the other side of the world, has provided the thrill, excitement and anticipation of that one: we were even invited to the flight deck and had some of the works explained to us.

From Las Palmas we made occasional bus trips to Maspalomas, then an area of rolling sand dunes going down to the sea, and only one hotel. Sadly the whole area has been developed, not everywhere in the best of taste. On one occasion we were returning to Las Palmas after swimming at Maspalomas and the bus was rather full; Megan and Irene found seats at the rear while Ralph and I stood near the front. Unbeknown to Ralph and I there was a group of young Scandinavians at the back who were celebrating with some liquid refreshment. Megan and Irene said later that it would have been rude to have refused an offer, so two happy and slightly unsteady ladies needed a hand to leave the bus at Las Palmas. Later on, the Canaries and Malta became firm favourites for Megan and myself, and through a friend in Las Palmas we had the use of an apartment for several winters, often spending two months there.

After Stanley emigrated to Australia, new horizons beckoned and we loved our visits there, which included stops in Hong Kong and Tasmania. To our regret we did not manage to get to New Zealand. Stanley and his partner Julia lent us their motor-caravan and we explored the Great Southern Ocean Road. One morning at Wilson's Promontory, the southernmost tip of Australia, I was in the caravan park toilet block and got into conversation with the fellow shaving next to me. Telling him where I lived in the UK I mentioned a "small place on the East Coast you have probably never heard of – Brightlingsea" he looked up, smiled and said "I keep my boat there!" I knew the boat but had never met the owner. Its a small world.

Megan had a relation by her first marriage who lived in Seattle, USA, and we enjoyed six weeks there in 1977, partly to travel, partly to stay with Peggy. We had time in Canada, spent ten days travelling across to Los Angeles, and saw the sights in New York, but missed the Statue of Liberty because we ran out of time!

Our caravan enabled us to cover not only most of England but also trips to Spain, Denmark and Sweden. We went to Dunnet Head in Scotland because Megan wanted to see if it really did stay light all midsummer's night, and we visited Ireland. Yes, Megan did hang upside down to kiss the Blarney stone!

What always astonished me on our trips abroad was the ability of foreigners to speak such good English. In Denmark, I apologised to one young man about my inability to speak any Danish and he quickly put me right: "It's a bloody awkward language, don't try it."

From the mid-nineties onward we started to enjoy holidays by coach. Apart from the UK we had holidays in Holland, Belgium, Germany, Switzerland and Italy — which was our favourite. On one of our journeys the coach driver took us over the St Gotthard rather than through the tunnel. It was beautiful weather and the journey breathtaking.

We took a ferry trip to Capri and though the sea was rough it was well worth the effort. During my time in Malta during the war I came across a book — The Story of San Michele by Dr Axel Munthe — in which he tells of how he discovered the island's beauty. Imagine my surprise to find myself standing outside his house, his name on a plaque and the balcony on the cliff face high above the blue sea below. Nearly sixty years between sharing his dream and experiencing some of its fulfilment. It was a moving moment.

So why weren't we sailing at this time? In 1986, several factors led us to sell the boat, including the death of Rick, Megan's son-in-law, in a mountaineering accident on Mont Blanc. We had also experienced three wet and windy summers, and the cost of maintenance and storage was increasing. Caravanning filled our time instead but in the following years, if we were walking along Brightlingsea Prom and the tide was full and the weather fair, we would often say "we still miss the water".

Megan and I had some wonderful journeys together, we found places before they became major tourist centres and we met friendly people wherever we were — in no small measure due to Megan's willingness to try to talk to them in their language. She was much better at it than I was.

Did we have a favourite destination? Yes, where the sun was warm, the sea benign, the locals friendly and the hinterland inviting. I am sure you all know and cherish such a place.

Honour of Being Deputy

As you get older, life invariably focuses close to home but it also brings many new and enjoyable opportunities.

In 1986 I was asked if I would like to become one of the six assistants to the Deputy of the Cinque Port Liberty of Brightlingsea. An historic civic position, the office of Deputy goes back more than 500 years and is part of the story of the Confederation of the Cinque Ports. Brightlingsea is not itself a Cinque Port but is a limb of Sandwich; the Deputy is a deputy of the Mayor of Sandwich and answerable to him in regard to the affairs and governance of the town and port of Brightlingsea.

A happy year – Megan and I as Lady Deputy and Deputy of Brightlingsea.

The Deputy is elected on choosing day (always the first Monday in December) by the Freemen of the town. He is confirmed in office by the mayor of Sandwich at Sandwich Guildhall in July, along with the deputies of Fordwich and Sarre in Kent, two other limbs of Sandwich. In the normal course of events the Deputy's senior assistant is proposed as the next Deputy, to be elected by the Freemen on choosing day if they agree, and in 1991 I had the honour of being elected Deputy and Megan became Lady Deputy.

A hectic and enjoyable year followed and we attended more than 120 events including opening bazaars and fetes, presenting prizes, judging at shows... and buying countless raffle tickets. One interesting highlight was the decision to restore the Deputy's Opal. This 3ins by 2ins jewel features a carving of a boat and is in a gold locket that hangs from the Deputy's chain of office. On the recommendation of the Victoria and Albert Museum, London, we had the opal restored at Garrards of Regent Street. To raise the money for the restoration, we held a Grand Opal Ball in the community centre. It was a wonderful occasion: black-tie, ball gowns and real dancing; waltzes, quick-steps and foxtrots. The Deputy's Opal is now insured for £5,000. I counted it a great privilege to be Mayor-Deputy.

Also at the end of the 1980s I was approached to see if I would like to become a freemason. After talking it over with Megan and friends who were masons, I was admitted to the Lodge of Faith. I had the good fortune to be installed as Master of the Lodge of Faith in 1997 and later served as Lodge Almoner. In 2001 I was granted a Provincial grand honour for my service to the lodge and to masonry. I am also a member of the Star in the East Lodge in Harwich, and in 2007 I had the honour of being elected Master there. Through masonry I have had the pleasure of friendships from wide-ranging backgrounds, my horizons have been extended and my understanding of human nature deepened. The philosophy of "brotherly love, relief and truth" has to me, more relevance than many of today's organised religions.

Brightlingsea Lunch Club has been important to me as well, and I was chairman for a year. The club aims to foster friendship among members and to support local organisations or individuals. We have helped young people with university and taking educational trips abroad, bought musical instruments and helped to fund Brightlingsea in Bloom to bring colour to the town in the summer. For many years we ran a hospital car service, taking the elderly and infirm to

Colchester and Clacton; the scheme wound up when Brightlingsea surgery began offering a more comprehensive service. The lunch club is men-only but at least once a year we have a ladies' evening, when wives, friend and partners are invited to dinner. Membership is professional and comprises mainly retired people.

A Thank-You

This autobiography was first published in 1993 as Memories, a booklet meant just for family consumption. Sixteen years on, and following proposals from various members of the family, this new edition has been published. There has been some elaboration, some deletions and some additions which I hope will add interest. As fragments of memory are unlocked, the editing could go on ad infinitum, but a halt must be called.

Thank you for reading my book, and I hope you have gained some pleasure from my ramblings. My sincere and heartfelt thanks go to all those who have helped me to enjoy my life, in particular the family, from grandparents to great-grandchildren. I have been fortunate to have experienced so much love and affection and support. It would have been a very dull life without your love and your laughter. Thank you!

RAYNER FAMILY TREE FROM 1766

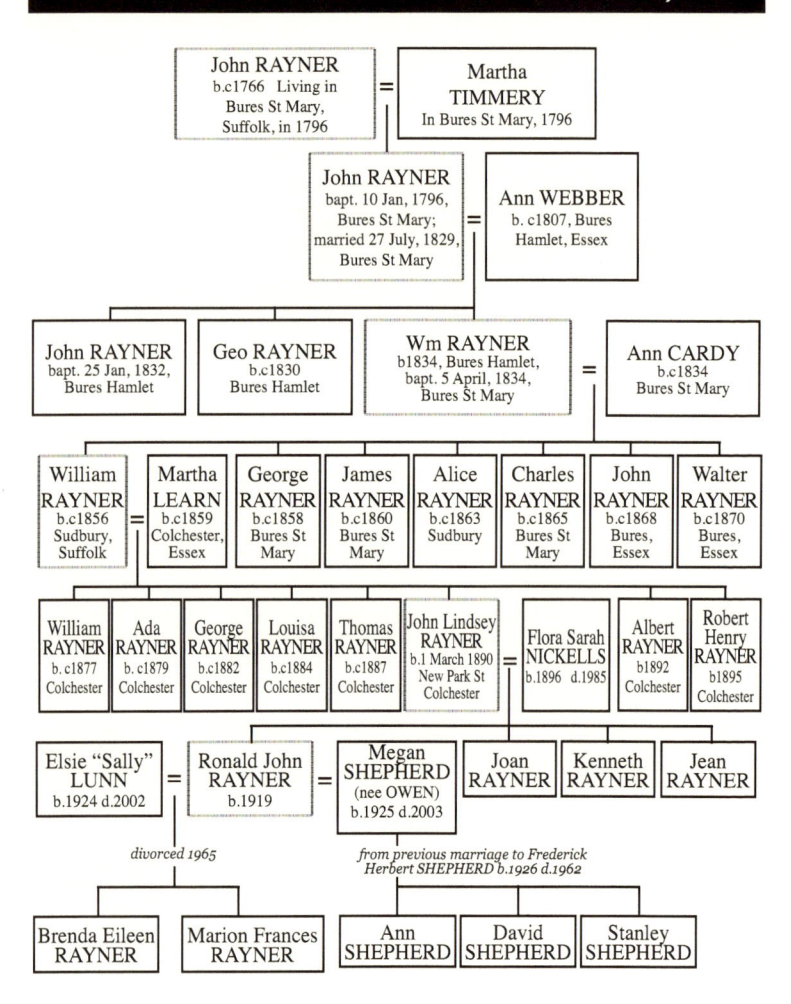

- John RAYNER b.c1766 Living in Bures St Mary, Suffolk, in 1796 = Martha TIMMERY In Bures St Mary, 1796
  - John RAYNER bapt. 10 Jan, 1796, Bures St Mary; married 27 July, 1829, Bures St Mary = Ann WEBBER b. c1807, Bures Hamlet, Essex
    - John RAYNER bapt. 25 Jan, 1832, Bures Hamlet
    - Geo RAYNER b.c1830 Bures Hamlet
    - Wm RAYNER b1834, Bures Hamlet, bapt. 5 April, 1834, Bures St Mary = Ann CARDY b.c1834 Bures St Mary
      - William RAYNER b.c1856 Sudbury, Suffolk = Martha LEARN b.c1859 Colchester, Essex
      - George RAYNER b.c1858 Bures St Mary
      - James RAYNER b.c1860 Bures St Mary
      - Alice RAYNER b.c1863 Sudbury
      - Charles RAYNER b.c1865 Bures St Mary
      - John RAYNER b.c1868 Bures, Essex
      - Walter RAYNER b.c1870 Bures, Essex
        - William RAYNER b.c1877 Colchester
        - Ada RAYNER b. c1879 Colchester
        - George RAYNER b.c1882 Colchester
        - Louisa RAYNER b.c1884 Colchester
        - Thomas RAYNER b.c1887 Colchester
        - John Lindsey RAYNER b.1 March 1890 New Park St Colchester = Flora Sarah NICKELLS b.1896 d.1985
        - Albert RAYNER b1892 Colchester
        - Robert Henry RAYNER b1895 Colchester
          - Elsie "Sally" LUNN b.1924 d.2002 = Ronald John RAYNER b.1919 = Megan SHEPHERD (nee OWEN) b.1925 d.2003
          - Joan RAYNER
          - Kenneth RAYNER
          - Jean RAYNER

divorced 1965

from previous marriage to Frederick Herbert SHEPHERD b.1926 d.1962

- Brenda Eileen RAYNER
- Marion Frances RAYNER
- Ann SHEPHERD
- David SHEPHERD
- Stanley SHEPHERD

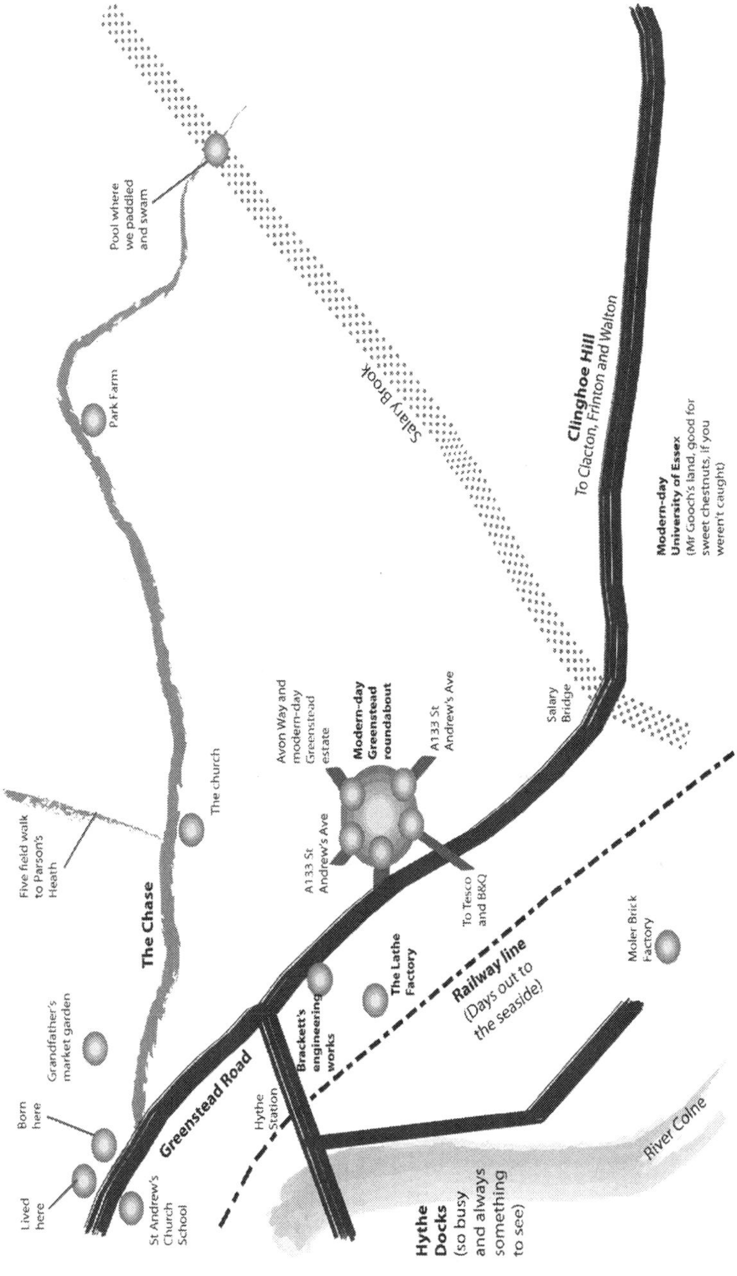

Pool where we paddled and swam
Park Farm
Salary Brook
Clinghoe Hill
To Clacton, Frinton and Walton
Modern-day University of Essex
(Mr Gooch's land, good for sweet chestnuts, if you weren't caught)
Salary Bridge
Avon Way and modern-day Greenstead estate
Modern-day Greenstead roundabout
A133 St Andrew's Ave
A133 St Andrew's Ave
To Tesco and B&Q
The church
Five field walk to Parson's Heath
The Chase
Grandfather's market garden
Born here
Lived here
St Andrew's Church School
Greenstead Road
Hythe Station
Brackett's engineering works
The Lathe Factory
Railway line
(Days out to the seaside)
Moler Brick Factory
River Colne
Hythe Docks (so busy and always something to see)

BIRCH
LEAF
BOOKS

birchleafbooks.co.uk

blurb.com